F
1219.3
.R38
L8

Luckert, Karl
W. 1934-

Olmec religion

WITHDRAWN

$14.95

DATE			

The Civilization of the American Indian Series

OLMEC RELIGION

OLMEC RELIGION

A KEY TO MIDDLE AMERICA AND BEYOND

by Karl W. Luckert

NORMAN
UNIVERSITY OF OKLAHOMA PRESS

Library of Congress Cataloging in Publication Data

Luckert, Karl W   1934–
    Olmec religion.

(The Civilization of the American Indian series; v. 137)
Bibliography: p.
Includes index.
    1. Olmecs—Religion and mythology. 2. Serpent-worship.
3. Indians of Mexico—Religion and mythology. 4. Indians of
Central America—Religion and mythology. I. Title. II. Series.
F1219.3.R38L8   299'.7   75–12869
ISBN 0–8061–1298–0

Olmec Religion is Volume 137 in *The Civilization of the American Indian Series.*

To my Chicago teachers—

Mircea Eliade

Joseph M. Kitagawa

Charles H. Long

PREFACE

Ever since I have become associated with history of religions I have noticed among my colleagues and friends a certain hesitancy in dealing with Middle American subject matters. My own response to Middle American religions was for many years one of helpless bewilderment. The categories of art and culture historians, useful as they may be for their specific purposes, have remained conspicuously barren for history-of-religions interpretations. Thus, with a background in the general history-of-religions field, I cannot boast of much specialized preparation in Middle American studies. In fact, this very study on Olmec religion began as something else.

During the summer of 1971 I succeeded in saving portions of the Navajo hunter tradition from oblivion. In the process of defining this earliest discernible stratum of Navajo religion, the over-all history of that religion came into better focus. I was also led into making a distinction between what might be archaic Apachean elements in that religion and what might be attributed to later Pueblo Indian influence. For the purpose of better identifying the Pueblo Indian portion in Navajo religion I turned my full attention to the former.

Among the many myths in Pueblo Indian religion the "myth of emergence" occupies the most central place. Briefly, it is an account of how the first ancestors of these people climbed into the surface world from a series of underworlds through a hole in the ground. The obvious intent of this myth is an allegory on human birth from Mother Earth. Upon a more careful examination, however, it becomes obvious that the primeval birth of men alone does not exhaust the ingredients of this myth.

A specialized study of the Pueblo Indian versions of the emergence myth proved as difficult as the limited study of Navajo ceremonialism had been earlier when I first became interested in American Indian religions. The reason for the difficulty was the same in both instances. Navajo ceremonialism, without knowledge of the earlier stratum of hunting rites, is a dazzling composite of cultural accretions. Likewise, the myths of the Pueblo Indians, without hints about their origination, development, and mergings in history, remain obscure puzzles. The obvious task at hand was therefore to trace the myth of emergence as far as historical investigations would carry.

By tracing the Pueblo Indian myth of emergence through one culture stratum after another I arrived at the earliest now clearly discernible stratum of Middle American civilization— the Olmecs. My first objective there was to do what many historians have been doing all along—to search the commentaries and to glean from them a few introductory pages to a broader study of Middle American civilization. In this task I failed. Several weeks I searched, compared, and was unable to get even a single page of coherent information on Olmec religion.

Only one way was left. I had to explore Olmec religious symbolism at some depth. Thus, what originally was begun as a brief introduction to the religious heritage of Middle America and the North American Southwest became a book in itself. In the course of writing it, many of my original questions about the Pueblo Indian emergence myth have been answered; some I must postpone for years of greater maturity.

For the existence of this book I owe thanks first of all to the National Endowment for the Humanities, for a 1972–73 fellowship to do research under the benign sponsorship of Professor Morris E. Opler at the University of Oklahoma. I thank all the people who have helped provide me with this span of free time. I appreciate the leave of absence from Northern Arizona University, and I thank all the members of my family for enduring a move to Norman and again back to Flagstaff.

For various helpful suggestions during the initial stages of this study, when the subject matter still centered on the Southwest, I am grateful to Richard J. Ambler of Northern Arizona University, to Barton A. Wright of the Museum of Northern

Arizona and to the staff of the library there. Various members of the anthropology department in the University of Oklahoma have on occasions given me information which had far-reaching consequences. The assistance given by a number of people at the University of Oklahoma Library is equally appreciated.

For the time when the study was at last narrowed to the Olmec problem, I acknowledge help by letter from Robert F. Heizer and I thank Michael D. Coe for his advice by telephone. These communications saved me needless travel time and expense in searching for various source materials.

A special word of thanks and appreciation goes to a group of scholars whom I never expected to get involved in a history-of-religions study—the herpetologists. Fascinated by serpents and unabashedly proud of their animals, these scholars and their serpents together fascinated me.

Frank Bryce of Cache, Oklahoma, was the first to pose his reptiles for this inexperienced photographer, though no pictures from this session could be rated a success. Charles C. Carpenter and several of his students at the University of Oklahoma corrected my ignorance about the life-styles of snakes on a number of occasions. I remember with great admiration the late Hobart F. Landreth, Jr., research director at the Oklahoma City zoo. On the day that I walked into his laboratory, I had never heard of the actual existence of "green" rattlesnakes. Nevertheless, after reading about the "green serpentine" La Venta mosaic masks I felt sure that there must be in existence green Mexican rattlesnakes with square faces and with clefts on their foreheads. Hobart Landreth suggested that I take a look at the South American Cascabel (Fig. 37). He regretted that his zoo did not have any other Mexican rattlesnakes at the time. I thank the staff of the zoo's herpetarium for making an unwilling Cascabel pose for me.

Herpetologists at the Natural History Museum of the University of Kansas took time out to show me a number of bottled Mexican snakes. No specimen satisfied the requirements better than the Cascabel—until one lucky day, in the zoo at Fort Worth, Texas, I found a genuine *Crotalus durissus durissus*. Mr. J. P. Jones, the herpetarium supervisor, graciously assisted me in my effort at photography.

During the months of ever new discoveries in the fall of 1972 I especially appreciated the free rein which I had over my time, as well as the good procedural advice of Professor Opler. Jerome Steffen, my colleague, with whom I shared an office, endured many an enthusiastic outburst of emotion. He was an excellent listener.

Charles Wicke graciously agreed to read the finished manuscript. To his observing eye the book owes a number of improvements. His lectures on Middle American archaeology at the University of Oklahoma brought significant comparative materials to my attention.

Then, during the summer of 1973, in Europe, I had the opportunity to converse about my discoveries and about the finished manuscript with a number of specialists and professors in the Middle and South American fields—with Werner Mueller and Thomas S. Barthel, Tuebingen; Bodo Spranz, Freiburg; Gerdt Kutscher and Anneliese Moennich, Berlin; Otto Zerries, Munich; and Heide Theisen, Vienna. My sincerest thanks go to all of them for their hospitality, their time, and their many helpful suggestions.

After my return to Flagstaff, the renewed conversations with Barton A. Wright about possible links between Middle America and the Pueblo kachina cult resulted in a few additions. It also became possible to include my own eye-witness report of the Hopi snake dance. Following several years of restrictions, non-Indians were admitted again in 1974 to the ceremonial at Shungopovi.

August, 1975   Karl W. Luckert
Flagstaff, Arizona

CONTENTS

OLMEC RELIGION

I

RELIGION AND CIVILIZATION

1. A New Approach

This book contains a new interpretation of the oldest religion in Middle American civilization. There were certainly religious people living in the New World prior to the Olmecs, but the Olmecs are now generally recognized as the first visible stratum of Middle American civilization, with the latest stratum being represented by the Aztecs, who flourished up to the time of the Spanish conquest. The history of Middle American religions in its entirety, from the Olmecs to the Aztecs, still escapes our grasp. But after this decipherment of essentials in Olmec religion, I am convinced that in the course of time the religions of many subsequent Middle American culture strata will be brought into better focus.

The studies which are presently available on Olmec religion are not primarily concerned with the subject "religion." The history of artistic expressions, seen in terms of stylistic changes, has received by far the majority of scholarly attention. This emphasis is a clear carry-over from the emphases in other Middle American arenas of study. Various inferences about Olmec religion, in addition to those of the art history approach, have been made on the basis of economic, sociological, and political generalizations. In all of these more or less scientific approaches, the essentials of Olmec religion have remained hidden and obscure.

The primary reason for this obscurity lies not in the difficult nature of Olmec religious art forms and symbols, but rather in the a-religious manner in which Western scholars work. With the age of the Enlightenment, Western minds became indeed enlightened about some things. Nature and matter were decoded as mechanical and impersonal processes; values, sanctions, and social structures were all credited to human genius and creativity. In the course of this kind of enlightenment the subject matter of religion—gods and other greater-than-human realities—was denied its ontological status. So the subject drifted into the keeping of literary critics and art historians who dealt with religious matters as if they were only creative constructs of the human imagination. In the history of Western scholarship the period of the Enlightenment corresponds therefore to a darkening—in the case of many scholars, even to an eclipse—of religious awareness. The scientific approach, control-oriented as it is, frequently blocks religious understanding among Western learned men. Control-mindedness and the religious attitude are opposites. This is why the historian of religions in many instances must reject both the methods and the conclusions of scientific men. Not that he is against science in principle; rather, he merely recognizes the limits of scientific controls in human phenomena, and in addition he suspects that the very success of the scientific disciplines and the populism which this success entails has obscured the presence of these limitations.

By trying to introduce the history-of-religions approach to Olmec religion, a subject matter to which it has not been applied before, I obviously owe to the reader a kind of systematic introduction. Since it must be brief, I therefore suspect that occasionally it will suffer from oversimplification. The reader who wishes to obtain a more thorough introduction to the history-of-religions approach in general is therefore advised to consult the works of Rudolf Otto, G. Van der Leeuw, Joachim Wach, and Mircea Eliade. My brief introduction to the discipline will not follow any of these men literally—"in spirit" it will be an approximation. I will try to express myself in terms and categories which have evolved and have proven useful in the course of several years of college teaching.

2. What is Religion?

Stated negatively, the historian of religions simply refuses to reduce the subject "religion" to the status of an appendix of economics, sociology, psychology, or any other academic discipline. For the purpose of this study "religion" is being defined as "man's response to so-conceived greater-than-human reality configurations." Whatever frightens man and whatever fascinates or overawes him is, when honestly faced, always something greater than man.

Most human religious responses are responses to greater-than-human personages or gods. This is so because, wherever "personhood" is being recognized as the quality which raises man above the animal level, there any so-conceived greater-than-human reality must possess at least the human quantity of personal qualities. While thus most religious responses of men tend to be responses to divine personages, not all responses need necessarily be that. What some greater-than-human reality configurations lack in personal qualities they seem to compensate for—at least for short time spans—in terms of sheer quantity and power. To such impersonal realities, as long as they are encountered as greater-than-human, man can only respond with anxiety and fear. Impersonal greater-than-human reality configurations are generally envisioned after a wave of scientific optimism has subsided—during which, allegedly, the personal greater-than-human realities of an earlier era have been broken down into less-than-human, impersonal and controllable, bits of reality. When a holistic vision of reality returns, it generally surprises mankind as a still impersonal but terrible avalanche of power. Nuclear energy, as it escapes in our time from the control of scientists into the hodgepodge of politics, is an example of this tendency in human history. Sooner or later man will either have to get a broader glimpse of reality, a religious view in which his personal qualities and needs are accounted for and can be included in his story of the greater whole, or he will have to suppress his religious insights and abandon himself more completely than ever to the pursuit of scientific controls. Guided by such self-imposed blinders, the scientific mind must then analyze every possible greater-than-human reality configuration which confronts it into less-than-human and controllable portions. It is obvious that the majority of the world's haunted people will never be able to join the cults of absolute despotism.

The religious and the scientific responses to so-conceived configurations of reality are direct opposites. At the same time, both types of responses are equally rational. Confronted by an inescapable greater-than-human reality, the only rational way is to acquiesce and to learn how to live submissively and in a state of religious dependence. On the other hand, when one is confronted by a number of small factors or variables, these can indeed be arranged rationally and controlled scientifically. In other words, I hold that it is as reasonable to pray to a personal greater-than-human reality as it is to do scientific experiments with impersonal less-than-human portions of reality.

Of course, there is an endless debate among men with regard to whether a given reality is a greater-than-human whole or a conglomeration of controllable variables. By appealing to reason alone, this debate will never be resolved one way or another. At this basic level man must follow convictions which lie deeper than his logic. He is sooner or later forced to draw somewhere from the great storehouse of mankind's unproven axioms. This is why many rational people today participate wholeheartedly in the established cult of scientific and technological exploitation of natural resources. At the same time, an ever-growing number of equally rational people oppose the scientific cult of control as it now operates and call their fellow men to responsibility toward humanity, ecology, and nature. All three of these last-mentioned categories have recently been discovered by people as greater-than-human, and therefore demanding, reality configurations. In an earlier era such realities were accepted by men as revelations and self-disclosures of gods. But labels, in the history of religions, are always secondary to ontology.

3. The Balance of Religion and Science

Religion and science, in this study, are looked upon as opposite mind-sets or attitudes, which are present in every culture and which in their basic functions do not differ from one culture to another. In every culture they represent the two opposite poles of the continuum of all possible human experiences. It is acknowledged that in the religio-scientific drama the actors, their make-up, the scenery of the stage, and even the script are being modified from one "scene" to another. But the content of the play never changes, namely, man's confrontation with greater-than-human reality configurations. Here a group of participants accepts bread and wine as clues to reality; there some meditate on the fact of nothingness. In the American Southwest some professionals make sand paintings, while on the island of Malekula Stone Age men have taken to the art of perfecting various geometric patterns of sand tracings—the one is to overcome illness, the other to overcome death. Here some devout men flee from the material world into monastic spirituality; there a great number of learned men ignore such spirituality and harness the elements of nature, which to them seem more real—all of this is being done in the pursuit of finding what is described as "the better life." Several millennia ago in Middle America a group of archaic maize planters rose into the horizon of civilization by carving designs in wood and stone.

The religio-scientific drama is always the same. Man wrestles with, conquers, or surrenders to, greater-than-human reality configurations. In the course of conquering such, man analyzes them into less-than-human components; he imposes faces and definitions and applies levers which seem to be rationally applicable to his various subject matters. In this manner, many uncertainties about life, many doubts about its ultimate meaning, are being checked. But there is no end to this drama. Beyond the expanded and controlled horizons of man dawn ever new configurations of reality which loom in greater-than-human proportions.

There have been "scenes" in this human drama where man rose up against greater-than-human reality configurations with the suicidal courage of Prometheus. It has seemed therefore at various points in human history as though a race of supermen had finally come of age. But then, with the same frequency, there have also been played in human history scenes in which the greatest of men have bowed to a greater-than-human will. They simply laid down their lives.

Both scenes, with their different extremes, have featured their own heroes. Wherever the hero of any extreme has obtained a following, his image has been transformed by the masses. In mystic identification with a hero, the follower imitates and eventually "becomes" his hero. This gradually changes the images of both the hero and of his followers. And so in this process, new victorious heroes become the hope of those whom they have defeated; suffering heroes become victorious in the end. Whether a hero is a powerful conqueror or whether he conquers in the long run by surrendering religiously, his appeal to the masses always involves a greater living space and a more authentic life which becomes possible within that wider horizon. Thus, along this continuum of human possibilities from scientific conquest to religious surrender, any human activity can, for periods of time, receive a soteriological meaning. Victorious heroes are revealed in games of war; suffering children of God are refined in the tortures of persecution; modern geniuses are found out when in scientific experiments their minds triumph over matter; enlightened Buddhists result when all of man's losing struggles are resolved as nothingness in nirvana; through the skillful use of instruments and chemicals our medical heroes prolong human lives. And then, death is overcome partially by merging harmoniously with the living processes of Nature; it is overcome more thoroughly by some who participate in the death/baptism and resurrection of Christ.

As much as man's beliefs and activities have varied in his pursuit of salvation and a better life, so the material media through which salvation has continually been symbolized have also varied. Men have been religiously fascinated by such soteriological symbols as sand paintings and tracings, by glittering jewels and gold (and by their modern paper substitutes), by blood, substitute victims, sacred texts, sacramental elements, chemical elements, tools and machinery, armory, nuclear energy, or by anything else which man has ever laid hands on and found beneficial. The ancient Olmecs had become fascinated by huge stones; and these stones, having been identified by them as greater-than-human entities *par excellence*, became the targets of the culture hero's activities. Later Middle American cultures have conquered megaliths further by reducing them to parts of large man-made masonry structures. The prominence of Olmec "schools" of sculptor-priests was in the process usurped by the great aristocratic landlords under whose sponsorship the large edifices were being built.

For every soteriological human activity man has known several ranks of culture heroes. First of all, there is the founder of a new Way. Frequently he is a wise man who began counseling balance to a world which was either too control-minded or which was hopelessly dependent on a threatening greater-than-human reality. Such a wise man generally sits at the center of everything and tries to balance the teeter-totter of his culture. There are times when for the sake of balance this man must lean toward the religious pole, and there are times when he must stretch toward the pole of scientific self-assertion. In the history of a culture, while one extreme is being downed, the other always rises in undetected vainglory. When finally, in the midst of their doom, the masses sense the futility of following one set of heroes, they look in the other direction. There, on the middle ground, they spot the wise man. Helplessly they flee toward him. Usually this wise man is overrun by the stampeding masses when he refuses to follow them all the way to the other extreme. Posthumously, when his pleas for balance can be more easily ignored, he may nevertheless be declared the hero of the new order. The dust raised by the stampede obscures for the time being the new cultural imbalance which is being produced. Notwithstanding this, some survivals of the wise man's teachings which pertain to cultural balance may for centuries keep the new order from becoming overly tyrannical. Theoretically speaking, if in the course of time the founder's vision of a balanced world were not lost by his followers, a tolerable balance could be maintained indefinitely.

But along come the culture heroes of the second and third generations. Together with the masses they have found salvation through the life of their founder. The unsought task of stabilizing the stampede has become theirs; they have to settle down to the priestly task of defining truths. Religious mediators of truth must systematize the practice of prayer and meditation; mediators of scientific truth must standardize their methods of analysis and experimentation. Life and thought, in either case, becomes ritualized. Rituals and methods, being in essence the same, stiffen and petrify at about the same speed. The time thus ripens for someone to discover again the lost dimension.

So far I have portrayed the teeter-totter of human culture in terms of either one extreme or the other. It is now time to add a significant qualification. There exist in this world no completely religious cultures, as also there exist no completely scientific cultures. At the very moment when a human society arrives at either of these extremes, it ceases to be. At the same time, one recognizes in our world many societies which are teetering excessively toward the pole of self-surrender or are tottering on the other side toward experimental self-extinction.

Complete religious submission forbids man to control, to kill, and to eat; without a measure of self-assertion toward at least some so-conceived less-than-human realities, man will die. In India, Mahavira and his Jain followers have moved as far as anybody to the religious extreme. They vowed *ahimsa* (not to injure and not to kill). Yet, in order to survive they had to compromise and to accept at least the fringe benefits of living in a society of cooks and butchers—they ate table scraps. Generalized religious submissiveness, while it made the medieval Western world a safer place to live in, also invited men of superhuman ambitions to play the role of God— to be God's representatives on earth, divine kings or judges.

Complete self-assertion and boundless passion which is directed only toward controlling things, when universalized, will boomerang and eventually destroy the controllers. Every conqueror produces victims artificially (scientists require "objects" or "subjects"). But, when for a period of time the victims have aspired to the ideals of their domineering heroes, they have themselves learned how to conquer. Generations of older conquerors will fall. In human societies this means revolution, in the natural world an ecology crisis develops, and in the science of physics, specifically, the control over carefully limited quantities of nuclear energy in the larger form of stock piles of bombs slips away into the dense jungle of politics. There in turn the harnessed energies appear to slip from the hands of political leaders only to boomerang toward the masses as general fear of a nuclear holocaust. Meanwhile, the propagation of laissez faire ideology in combination with scientific methodology has in fact liberated men from an institutionalized and occasionally tyrannical greater-than-human reality, the church. But this same drive for liberty and experimentation is now bent on freeing a mass of people for nothing more than to tinker with the earth and with every aspect of the societal order. Given the continuation of this development, at some point in the future all societal checks and balances could be eroded—unless, in the meantime some god appears and fascinates the people into a new order.[1]

What a human culture can hope for is its survival in a state of relative tranquillity, somewhere between the two extremes. The condition, where each man does not claim for himself more privileges than he allows the other fellow to have, is perhaps an unobtainable Utopian dream. But dreamers of that dream, spokesmen for balance and justice, have been heard of in every known culture. I am therefore convinced that in one form or another this dream of balance between scientific self-assertion and the religious awareness of dependence was also dreamed by some Olmec wise men. Had this not been the case, their cultural effort would not have held together through the number of centuries that it has. Nevertheless, every bit of balance in human culture must be labored for. Olmec sculpture pieces are lasting memorials of a scientific and priestly struggle against greater-than-human powers—as these powers have been traced to and captured in mysterious blocks of basalt. There is strong evidence that, at a time when the sculptured or "domesticated" greater-than-human

---

[1]I happen to be convinced that man-made laws will never awe men into conformity, much less will the experimental laws of scientific specialists, or controls imposed by a police system. If laws are to be effective, they must be deducible directly from some generally cultivated greater-than-human vision of reality. Western laws and rights, for example, have traditionally been deduced from the will of God and from the order of Nature. Legislators at their best have been discoverers. Thus, any future authority in the Western world which is less comprehensive than God and Nature will not hold the dike against individual experimentation.

basalts had become too intimately linked with the aristocratic ambitions of some Olmec sculptor-priests, a more democratic reform movement took the wind out of the priests' sails. The timely discovery of a new kind of greater-than-human reality configuration—green serpentine rock—helped justify among the reformers the destruction of symbols which were representative of the previous order that had become oppressive. As usually happens, the Olmec reformers overshot the balance. Balance was never regained in their culture. The seeds of the Olmec experience were thus scattered and bore fruit elsewhere and in successive strata of the great Middle American civilization.

II

HOW TO MEET THE OLMECS

1. In Recognition of the Jaguar

The jaguar, the animal which in books and essays and in every discussion of Olmec religion has to this day been the central figure, shall be honored in this study only by way of a brief introductory section (Fig. 1). At the outset it shall be admitted that pre-Columbian Middle America had in its later periods a widespread jaguar cult. It shall be acknowledged further that this cult, along with that of the eagle, was clearly established at the time from which derives the ideological pattern of the Codex Borgia. Beyond this, it is possible that some Middle American tribes, contemporaries of the Olmecs, or late Olmecs at Chalcatzingo, who were still close to the life-style of hunters, had a jaguar cult. And finally it shall be acknowledged that in the course of the twentieth century the jaguar figure has fascinated and even inspired a number of Western scholars. But, what has not been proven to my satisfaction in the published reports is the assertion that there was a jaguar cult among the first agricultural Olmecs. The Olmec jaguar which has been identified by archaeologists, artists, and culture historians—as far as can presently be traced at the major ceremonial sites—does not seem to me to be there.[1]

---

[1]The only Olmec-type faces with feline features, of which I am aware, belong to two figures of the Dumbarton Oaks collection and to a head at the Museo Nacional de Antropología (see Benson, 1968, pp. 146f.). Feline claws are also present on the Potrero Nuevo Monument 3. All of these I regard as post–La Ventan styles. The two Chalcatzingo jaguar reliefs, published in Benson, 1972, are apparently late Olmec; moreover, serpent tongues

Fig. 1.—Jaguar.

It is now difficult to establish who first named an Olmec monument a jaguar. Perhaps it began with Saville in 1929 when he described an Olmec carved axe as "the conventional mask of a tiger" (Joralemon, 1971, p. 5). Perhaps it all started with the jade figurine which was found in 1909 at Necaxa, in the mountains of northeastern Puebla (Fig. 2). George Vaillant in his essay of 1932 (pp. 512 ff.) identified this 3.25-inch-high jade figure as a "tiger, properly speaking ocelot or jaguar." In the same article Vaillant also related other Olmec faces to this

abound on these figures. Perhaps these reliefs signify a point in Olmec history when shamanic leaders, possessed by jaguar tutelaries from an earlier hunting culture, captured the planters' cult of the Serpent. Also, it is entirely possible that Olmec religion already proceeded by a dual calendar—with summer and maize planting under the tutelage of the Serpent, and winter with the activity of hunting under the tutelage of the traditional guardians of shamans: under jaguars, eagles, and other divine exemplary predators.

"tiger." In the early days this identification was reasonable enough. A crouching beast in this position could very well be a humanized jaguar. We must remember that Saville and Vaillant did not have available a collection of evolutionary prototypes for their "tigers." Today this figure stands toward the end of a long line of crouching Snake men; its bare gums and the split tongue designs at its skirt put it safely into this category. In the early days, when not many Olmec monuments had been found, gigantic Aztec stone tigers stood in

Fig. 2.—Necaxa, Puebla: tiger-mouth jade figurine. *(Courtesy American Museum of Natural History)*

15

museums for everyone to see. Thus, as happens so often in archaeological research, the sequence in which the Middle American faces have been found has obscured their original meaning.

In 1939, when Matthew Stirling began his large-scale project of excavating Olmec sites, his expectancy was already slanted in favor of finding jaguars. In his 1943 publication, twelve jaguar representations are identified. After examining his evidence, I believe that seven of these are serpents; for the remaining five insufficient information is available for calling them either "jaguars" or "serpents." Not that Stirling can be accused of blindly naming jaguars. In describing his "zoomorphic altar" of Izapa he called it "a crouching animal, evidently a jaguar, although some elements of the face seem more like a serpent" (Fig. 23, No. 3). The pioneer Olmec archaeologist, when he formulated this description, was looking right at the key to Olmec religion. His generosity in giving the name "jaguar" to creatures with split tongues must be understood against the background of academically established facts. His inference concerning "worship of a jaguar being" among the Olmecs (1943, p. 3) must be appreciated in the same context.

According to his 1952 field report on La Venta, Philip Drucker saw "jaguar-monsters" everywhere. To his credit it must be said, however, that when he referred to the split-tongued jaguar-monster of the sarcophagus, he added this significant sign—?—clear evidence of his having had second thoughts (Fig. 23, No. 25). In a section specifically dedicated to jaguar-monsters and jaguars (pp. 192 ff.), he analyzes their facial features into component parts. Flat-bottomed noses in all of his examples, a split tongue, and two sets of split fangs, are present in his jaguar inventory. A few pages later, nevertheless, he notes the absence of the serpent motif in Olmec art. The reptilian attributes of the jaguar-monster, Drucker reasoned (I suspect under the influence of Miguel Covarrubias), have no relation to the Mayan plumed serpent theme. His summary of Olmec religion is therefore that a "considerable theologic and ceremonial difference" existed between the Mayas and the Olmecs.

The joint report on the 1955 excavations at La Venta (Drucker, Heizer, and Squier, 1959), while it introduced some

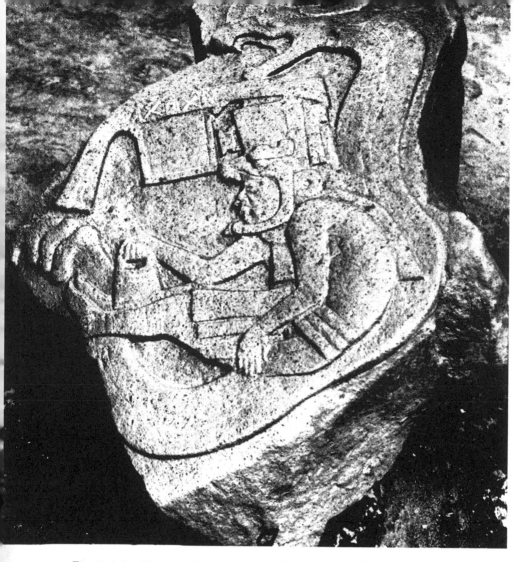

Fig. 3.—La Venta: Monument 19. *(Courtesy Smithsonian Institution)*

new monuments, primarily set out to deepen our knowledge with regard to Complex A architecture. The famous "pavement mosaics" have in the process been identified as "jaguar masks." How hazily, meanwhile, the notion of the "plumed serpent" has been applied in the interpretation of Olmec monuments is perfectly illustrated in the description of Monument 19 (Fig. 3). This "strictly realistic representation" is

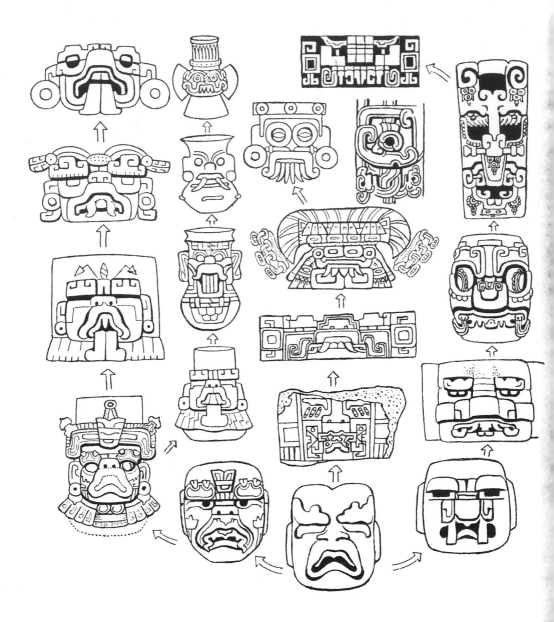

Fig. 4.—Chart "showing Olmec influence on evolution of the jaguar mask into rain gods." From *Indian Art of Mexico and Central America*, by Miguel Covarrubias. *(Copyright © 1957 by Alfred A. Knopf, Inc., reprinted by permission of the publisher)*

said to be a "plumed rattlesnake." It is seen to establish "the occurrence of the Feathered Serpent as a theme in Olmec art . . . though not a common one." Approaching the subject matter from a different perspective, I wonder about this interpretation. The rattlesnake I can see; I can also see its exaggerated head scales. But where are the plumes? Historically speaking, the subject matter of this monument signifies rather the later transferral of a Snake man from the mouth of the Serpent (compare below, Chapter VI) into his bodily embrace. It signifies a late stage in religious development at which men and serpent gods have become partners.

The archaeological reports which I have mentioned do not pretend to be interpretative syntheses. Even though some of their unfortunate labels have generated misinterpretations later on, the immense body of good data which has been made available through them is priceless. The authors deserve our most sincere praise and appreciation. My task now is to interpret the data as a whole. Thus, in reading the archaeological reports attentively I have been able to detect in their interpretational suggestions and nomenclatures occasional traces of one man in particular—Miguel Covarrubias.

The late Miguel Covarrubias has recently been honored by Ignacio Bernal with the title "The Last of the Olmecs" (1969, p. *v*). Michael Coe described him as a professional artist and a man with "enormous intellect and tremendous enthusiasm. . . . no other person could rival him in his intuition about the Mesoamerican past and in his feeling for objects and styles" (1968, p. 47). Knowing this charismatic man only through his pale reflections in books, I am nevertheless intrigued by him as the man who seems to have been the cause of enthusiasm for so many Olmec scholars. As far as Covarrubias' sense for Olmec objects and styles is concerned, I, too, am convinced that he has no rival. His chart of style sequences, from Olmec faces to later Middle American representations of gods, is important, even though I do not agree with his idea of the basic Olmec religious vision (Fig. 4).

Judging from the interpretations of my predecessors I surmise that, had I been under the direct spell of the living Covarrubias, my reinterpretation of Olmec religion might never have taken place. Enchanted by this great man, I will refrain from contesting the title which was coined in his honor. Nevertheless, Covarrubias was a new kind of Olmec. Fascinated by a post-Olmec greater-than-human reality, he has inspired in our century a healthy neo-Olmecian enthusiasm which has carried the scholarship of that field to its present height. Archaeologists, culture historians, and even this historian of religions are indebted to him.

When Covarrubias looked at Olmec iconography and art, he found that some faces "are clearly human, others have a fantastic, haunting mixture of human and feline characteristics in varying degrees. It is often difficult to guess whether a given carving was intended to represent a man disguised as a jaguar or a jaguar in the process of becoming a man" (Covarrubias, 1957, p. 50). While thus the man never wondered about an alternative to the Olmec jaguar, there were many reasons why such doubts were really unnecessary: "It is easy to understand this jaguar obsession in the mystic solitude of the jungle, which is like a tall, green cathedral, where every noise, every rustle of leaves, every distant crackling of broken twigs brings to mind the presence of the dreaded man-eater. To the ancient Indians the jaguar was a symbol of supernatural forces—not a simple animal, but an ancestor and a god."

While Covarrubias wondered occasionally about such difficulties as bare gums in these jaguar mouths, his answers outnumbered his questions generally in a ratio of two to one: "The toothless mouth is significant because it lacks the jaguar's most important feature. This could be interpreted in two ways: either it represents the face of a humanized jaguar cub or it is the flayed face of a jaguar to be used as a mask" (1957, p. 59). Apparently he never noticed the reptile which still has these toothless gums.

To explain the development from Olmec jaguars to serpentlike deities which, he admitted, ruled in later Middle America, Covarrubias postulated the influence of a mythical "sky dragon" and a "serpent X" (1957, pp. 60ff). The post-Olmec development of jaguars into serpentlike beings, as illustrated by his chart, "could have been caused by misunderstanding of the original significance of the symbols by artists of later epochs." Why artists who were removed from the Olmec era by only a few centuries should already have drifted farther from the original intent than a twentieth-century artist goes unexplained.

To Covarrubias goes the credit for systematizing the problems which remain for future Olmec scholars to ponder (Covarrubias, 1957, p. 53). Five problems remain: the age of Olmec civilization; the relationship between early preclassic peasants and aristocratic Olmecs; the contrast between exquisite jades, along with monuments of the Gulf Coast, and simple preclassic pottery; the meaning of the "strange Olmec traits" and the identity of their creators; and finally, whether Olmec culture really was the mother culture of Middle America. A clearer answer to all of these questions, with the exception of the problem of general chronology and racial membership, will be possible from this study on Olmec religion.

Walter Krickeberg, who in 1961 published an excellent summary of the major Middle American religions, shows in his section on the Olmecs a strong dependency on Covarrubias. This influence is already evident in Krickeberg's earlier work on Old Mexican cultures (1956). Beyond this, Krickeberg draws support from Haeckel's *"Der Herr der Tiere im Glauben der Indianer Mesoamerikas."* At this point it seems to me that Krickeberg was carried away by the overpowering force of the jaguar motif; as a result he began to reason on the terms of a hunter religion. But how can a jaguar-oriented hunter religion explain the life of Olmec maize planters? Covarrubias had already passed over this issue: "This jaguar fixation must have had a religious motivation, either totemic or related to the cult of the early rain and earth spirits conceived as jaguars" (Covarrubias, 1957, p. 58). At this point I fail to see clearly how Covarrubias and Krickeberg managed to explain the transition from a hunter to a planter culture. A jaguar for a primary rain god or earth spirit? This is difficult to envision. Jaguars, like all the great felines, have fascinated hunters, warriors, and aristocrats, and as far as I have been able to determine, they have managed only to annoy the agriculturists. Fortunately there appears to be an easier solution to the problem of Olmec "jaguars."

Michael Coe has published an illustrated book entitled

The Jaguar's Children (1965 a). He identifies these "children" in the descriptive style of Covarrubias, as "werejaguar babies, offspring of feline father and human mother, deities of thunder, lightning, and rain. . . . their jaguar ancestry shows only in the down-drawn corners of the mouth." As an example of a werejaguar baby the author shows the famous thumb-sucking child figure in the Museum of Primitive Art. In my judgment, the down-drawn corners of the mouth owe more to a serpent than to a jaguar. In addition, the diamond patterns and stripes on the back of the figure link it even more closely with the world of snakes. Admittedly, the symbolism of this figure alone is inconclusive. The accumulative evidence of this study will help the reader to decide the question. Coe's excavations at San Lorenzo, to the extent that they have been published, have been most valuable for this study. To his book, *America's First Civilization* (1968), I owe my first excitement about the Olmec phenomenon.

In 1969 Ignacio Bernal summarized the "Olmec World" and speculated on the presence or absence of "formal" divinities in Olmec religion. I do not feel qualified to discuss the distinction between formal and other divinities—mainly from lack of comprehending what this distinction means. My study here is based on observation of given religious symbols; I shall dare to interpret them only as far as my limited powers of reason and personal empathy will carry me. And it is at this level of concrete symbols that I meet again, in Bernal's work, the jaguar's name which I feel does not belong.

In his historical interpretation, Bernal, drawing from Kirchhoff, compared the Olmec jaguar with the later struggles between Aztec Eagle knights and Aztec Jaguar knights. Their respective hostilities are explained as the result of ideological change on the one hand and the persistence of the archaic jaguar symbol on the other: the jaguar was the god of early Mesoamerican cultures and the eagle the deity of more recent ones. I personally see no evidence of such a development. Both Jaguar and Eagle cults, so it seems to me, intruded later and perhaps in connection with the rise of militarism into the serpent cult of the maize planters. It is quite conceivable that both Jaguar and Eagle cults were spawned directly from hunters' secret societies; thus they may have remained unaffected by agriculturist ideology. Agriculturists, nevertheless, fell victim to these increasingly more aristocratic cults.

Then in 1971, elaborating on Michael Coe's identification of six different types of Olmec gods from the year 1968, P. D. Joralemon picked up the problem of Olmec religion by doing a systematic analysis of iconographic elements. With a graphic "vocabulary" of 182 components from sacred Olmec sculptures and designs he arrived at the revised number of ten different Olmec gods. The most important Olmec deity, god "number one," is the "jaguar-dragon."

From an art historian's perspective this approach to Olmec iconography makes good sense. It yields an impressive volume of exact details. Precision and the ability to control multiple facts are virtues of the scientific mind. In contrast, however, the historian of religions knows in his far-flung manner that ten gods are neither generated by men nor out of a vacuum. Greater-than-human reality configurations are discovered only by people who honestly seek to meet them or who are ideologically prepared to recognize them. The historian of religions also knows that the artistic representations of a single deity can take six, ten, or a hundred different forms. For example, were Joralemon's method of classifying iconographic components applied to Christianity, we would certainly arrive at a dozen different Christs—at least that many different halos and crowns have been put on the central figure of Christendom. The historian of religions also knows that ten unrelated gods will never generate a unified culture. The continuity of subject matter in Olmec artifacts and edifices points unmistakingly to a single fascination. Thus, the differentiation of gods, as Joralemon in the end himself suggests, has indeed been a premature effort. It may be said at this point, that a differentiation of Olmec divine personages can proceed on a sounder basis after the primary Olmec religious vision has been decoded.

For an absolutely necessary first step, before we can proceed with identifying any more Middle American gods, I suggest that a photographic survey be made of all Mexican serpents, lizards, and amphibians. We need full-face portraits of all these plus illustrations of bodily shapes and skin markings. I am now convinced that many so-called "abstract" art forms of Middle America are realistic copies of divine animals which are still around. Even a good portrait of a live jaguar could have prevented some mistakes in the past. Late stone tigers may carry more prestige in archaeology and in museums, but the shapes of living jaguars are far more archaic and precise.

The scholar who in my estimation came closest to solving the Olmec mystery is Peter Furst. In his essay, "The Olmec Were-Jaguar Motif in the Light of Ethnographic Reality" (1968), he has, on the basis of sound comparisons, called into question the jaguar of the ancient Olmecs. Had more materials from the general history of religions been available to him, and had he dissociated himself from the heat of the debate, this anthropologist could have pushed the Olmec "jaguar" over the brink. I discovered his essay when the first draft of this book had already been written. My own suggestion— that the jaguar as a religious symbol may literally have "leaped upon" a popular Serpent cult when leaders of hunter societies, jaguar-shamans, captured the priesthood of the Great Serpent—is very much supported by his evidence on the "jaguar-shaman transformation complex." His findings are also in harmony with my own observations, which I made earlier, concerning "prehuman flux" in the Navaho hunter tradition. The recently published jaguar reliefs from Chalcatzingo (Benson, 1972), which are loaded with snake symbols and which show felines seizing upon human beings, seem to indicate shamanistic jaguar transformations and visions among late or even post-Olmec priests.

Over the past two decades a considerable debate has developed concerning what Michael Coe has called "the sin of Bayer, Saville, and Vaillant" (1968, p. 42). These gentlemen have named the Olmecs after the land of rubber trees in which they lived. This "sin" must now be re-evaluated as a stroke of good fortune. Had scholarship taken earlier to Jiménez Moreno's suggestion, of switching to the name "Tenocelome" (those of the tiger mouth), we probably would have had the jaguar's ghost haunt the ancient Olmec people in our books forever (Jiménez Moreno, 1966, p. 7). I still can think of no better name for the bearers of Middle America's oldest stratum of civilization than the name which links them with the land in which they lived. If we wish to distinguish them from present-day groups which inhabit the land of rubber, all we need to do is add occasionally an adjective and call them the "ancient Olmecs."

2. The Meaning of Megaliths

Megaliths, or simply, man-placed "large stones" have been found in many parts of the world. Their significance elsewhere may shed some light on their meaning in Olmec religion. I shall therefore discuss briefly how the interpretation of megalithic monuments has fared elsewhere. After a wave of overly enthusiastic decoding of megalithic monuments earlier in this century, Heine-Geldern restated in 1959 the "megalith-problem" on a more sober basis. He rejected the then prevalent explanation that sun worshipers from Egypt in search of gold and pearls spread across the world and disseminated the practice of working with large stones. We may add that this kind of interpretation has been nurtured among some scholars by a general pan-Egyptian enthusiasm at a time when sensational discoveries were being made in Egyptian archaeology. The inference about the meaning of large stone monuments was then drawn somewhat in this manner: the Egyptians built large stone monuments; they also worshiped a sun god; therefore, sun worship goes along with large stone construction. In accordance with this kind of logic, the ghosts of sun worshipers were detected behind man-placed boulders throughout the world.

Heine-Geldern's reassessment is more humble. He lists a variety of ideological associations which have been made by different peoples in relation to their megaliths. Among these are world perspectives which are oriented to genealogies, eschatological beliefs, and even to a sky god now and then. But "wherever megalithism is found flourishing, a well-developed ancestor cult is always present" (Heine-Geldern, 1959, p. 164). Emphasizing after the manner of Heine-Geldern the data from Oceania, the link between megaliths and ances-

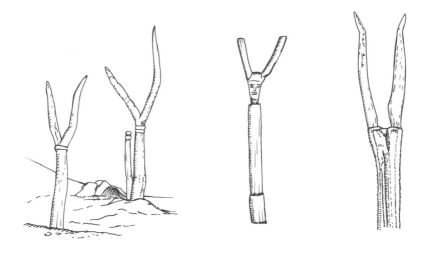

Fig. 5.—Ceremonial forked posts. Left: Sudan. Center: Nias. Right: India. *(Drawn after Heine-Geldern, 1959)*

tor cults is indeed supported. Riesenfeld (1950, p. 667) documented this relationship for Melanesia.

A little later in his essay Heine-Geldern has found it necessary to drastically reduce his definition of "megalithism," so much so that for our present purpose it loses all meaning. According to him Inca large stone monuments, for example, are no longer megalithic. Presumably this wipes out also the related Middle American megaliths. The authority of V. G. Childe, which Heine-Geldern evoked at this point, does not help us avoid the ambiguity of having nonmegalithic large stones. He says, "The basis of classification is not merely material and magnitude, but also function." This modification, unfortunately, demolishes the category "megalithic" for initial approaches to all prehistoric cultures. Horst Nachtigall (1958) has returned to the simpler terminology according to which all large stones, Inca, Mexican, and others, are megaliths. But then, with regard to Olmec megaliths, Nachtigall could do little in that particular study beyond recataloguing the interpretations which were already in the books.

To Heine-Geldern's list of megalith-related ideologies we must add, for the sake of Middle America, another important one—the cult of the Serpent. Accordingly, ancestor worship may or may not always be strong in megalithic cultures. This revision does not mean that the megalithic builders of our world share no common ideological orientation. Serpent worship in Middle America and ancestor worship in Oceania both belong to the culture stratum of paleoplanters. The practice of agriculture is still new, and on this stage man has to reorient his thinking from a hunter's world to the reality pattern of controlled plant growth—large scale seeding, fertilization, growth, and killing at harvest time. To better understand their world, these planters have watched closely the earth on which they so obviously depended. Boulders, serpents, the buried or "planted" dead, as well as the people yet to be born, were all discovered as belonging to that reality complex of earth and vegetation. And with this reality configuration are also associated the powers of darkness, light, weather, and climate.

In one section of his essay Heine-Geldern has summarized a broad range of information about the megalith-related *Gabelpfaehle* or "forked posts" (1959, pp. 174f.). The occurrence of such forked posts has been reported from Nias, Flores, Sumba, Timor, New Guinea, Melanesia, Polynesia, Madagascar, and many parts of Africa (Fig. 5). In some places these forked posts are associated with the horns of bovines; generally they are interchangeable with menhirs. In many traditions they are remembered as posts to which sacrificial victims—often cattle—were tied. But, as Heine-Geldern recognizes, the distribution of forked posts far exceeds the habitats of cattle or even of horned animals. Forked sticks are therefore not necessarily limited to representing sets of horns. At the same time, Olmec religion may give us a hint about a possible original meaning of forked monuments. Their most elementary meaning is not difficult to decipher; they mean what they look like—"one becomes two." For the paleoplanter this was a symbol of plant growth; in addition, human growth derived from plant growth. The "one becomes two" symbol is what helped the ancient planters of Middle America link maize agriculture with serpents (see below, Figs. 18–21, 52).

The serpent's split tongue and the use of forked posts for fastening sacrificial animals match well with the Middle American cult of the hungry Earth Serpent. Thus it may well be the case that among the megalithic cultures of the world precisely the Middle American, which has hitherto been treated as an unrelated stepchild, has something to offer in the way of explaining some of the others.

While I have thus modified the "megalith problem," it has been done solely from the necessity which the Middle American situation has dictated. I still feel very much indebted to Heine-Geldern's imaginative writings. So for instance, his essay on two distinct ancient world perspectives (1957) contains a more fortunate set of generalizations on the subject of megalithism. The cosmic-magic world view, where groups of people see themselves in relation to the greater cosmos and its far-flung agencies, is contrasted with the genealogical or megalith-related view of the world. The union of male and female principles is seen as the basic creative reality of the genealogical world view.

In its broad outline I accept this distinction of the two types of world views. Nevertheless, since it is the case that both the "cosmic" and the "genealogical" views of the world sooner or later tempt man to the magical assertion of human over divine power, I prefer to call the first type simply "cosmos-oriented." With regard to the other type, I feel that "genealogical" refers too strongly to ancestors; for an alternative I recommend "earth-oriented." Earth-related and earth-dependent is the livelihood of the planters. Buried in the earth are the ancestors. In the earth and in water dwell most of their gods—and various kinds of serpents.

To the earth also belong megaliths—at least up to that moment in history when human effort has stacked them sufficiently high for men to risk their abortive leaps and climbings to a higher plane. When that stage is reached, individual large stones are no longer of primary importance; instead, human constructs and designs have then usurped the centrality of individual sacred boulders. Megalithism, an earth-oriented religious attitude, has at that stage become megalithic science—civilization. In the construction of their "Babylonian towers" men have taken full control. Great monuments, of the kind which score in our history books, symbolize above all else the greatness of human efforts. They are the debris which remains behind after man is through fighting his wars with the gods. An ancient generation of greater-than-human realities, or gods, has been modified by sculptors and has subsequently been arranged by builders into monuments of human greatness. This quest for civilization is never over. Beyond the ruined imagery of the previous age, ever new greater-than-human reality configurations appear. Prometheus will try to conquer them no matter what their guises. And then, Prometheus and his followers will accept the consequences and will suffer.

3. Olmec Historiography

While the primary objective of the present effort is an interpretation of Olmec religious symbolism, a minimum amount of historical work cannot be escaped. I shall do my best to establish historical sequences; at the same time, I believe that the religious interpretations given in this book represent a greater degree of certainty. The feeling of slight discomfort with regard to the former can be traced, psychologically perhaps, to the fact that on several occasions I have felt it necessary to discount the views of full-time archaeologists and historians. Inspired by my discoveries pertaining to Olmec religious symbolism, the wings of enthusiasm have, perhaps, carried me too far afield into the neighboring territory of historiography. A scholarly and safe book could have been written on the more obvious aspects of Olmec iconography alone; but such caution has never been among my virtues.

The sequential outline of four La Venta "phases," as presented by Drucker, Heizer, and Squier (1959, pp. 121 ff.), is to a large extent based on stratigraphic evidence. My only objection to the published stratigraphic information is that it is horizontally discontinuous. Without some very substantial imaginary jumps it has been impossible for me to trace the construction of the La Venta "Complex A" from the bottom

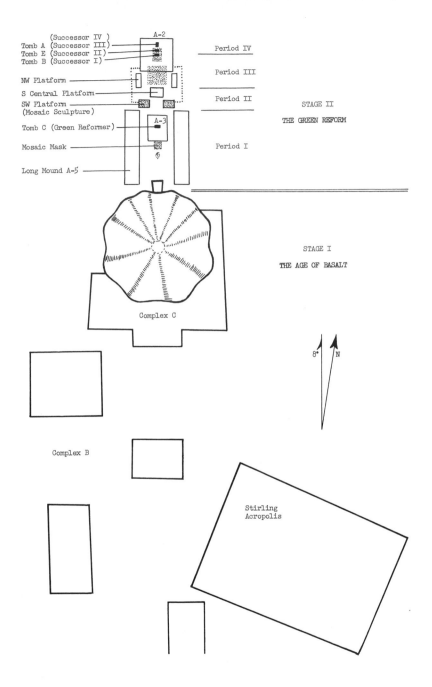

Fig. 6.—Historical map of La Venta.

up. This objection is linked directly to my builder's instinct and distrust of the stratigraphic method as a primary tool for unraveling large areas. Presumably, if builders of an earlier generation had access to fill or clay of a certain color, later generations could have obtained these materials also.

The area which has been lumped together for excavation as "Complex A" is approximately 250 feet wide and 600 feet long. Discounting for the moment the small platform at the north side of the great pyramid, this area contains three distinct groups of surface structures with three structures contained in each group (Fig. 6). These structures vary in length from about 280 feet to 30 feet; they vary from simple surface mounds to depth constructions which reach over twenty feet into the ground. Moreover, the three groups, of three surface structures each, vary considerably in size. The proportions balanced to one another in terms of distances and dimensions in each group are very obvious.

The only exception in this three-stage uniformity appears in the third group of Complex A. The Northeast and Northwest platforms do not match the immensity of Mound A–2. But here it must be pointed out that originally the masses of this triad of mounds stood in a good balance. Mound A–2 was a small burial mound at first. From a historical perspective, the enlargement of Mound A–2 marks a new era. Because no other structural remains have survived from this "era," I shall distinguish it in my outline below merely as a final "period"—Period IV of Stage II.

That a complex site the size of La Venta has been constructed from the bottom up according to a single plan seems virtually impossible. I have yet to find a city or temple compound in the entire world where the basic horizontal layout has not been altered, say, in three generations of active construction. I recognize that there is a good chance for floor plan stability over a number of generations in a single vertical structure, such as a Gothic cathedral or even the La Venta pyramid. For the latter I suspect several centuries of periodic vertical growth. But the area which extends north of the La Venta pyramid is different. It shows unambiguously that there has been horizontal northward planning and development.

Along with bypassing the major portion of stratigraphic

data I shall also have to ignore the available radiocarbon dates. These dates, with an average margin of error plus or minus three hundred years, can easily be identical with each other. A range of six hundred possible years for a single date amounts to over twice the time which I suspect it took for starting construction in the Complex A area, for completing it, and for abandoning it. Beyond that, if certain radiocarbon approximations are linked with a discontinuous stratigraphy, the entire construct collapses. I personally prefer therefore the old-fashioned method of geometric and stylistic comparison. And indeed, if read from south to north, the archaeological remains north of the great pyramid read like the well organized Part Two of a picture book. This Part Two is made up of four "chapters" or periods. The time covered by Part Two of this archaeological picture book is measurable as horizontal movement from south to north by five, possibly six, generations of ceremonial chiefs.

Part One of the La Venta picture book cannot be written yet as well as the last portion. From the Complex B and the Complex C areas, and from the remainder of the island, only scanty information is available. It is possible that "Chapter One" of La Venta's "Part One" would have to begin at the south end of the island with Stirling's sandstone monuments A, B, and C (Fig. 7). From the present shape of the map, which shows only the central portion, I suspect that at least two more "chapters" will some day result from complexes B and C alone. The Stirling Acropolis simply does not match the rest.

Whatever future excavations may reveal about this area, for the time being I must combine all of Part One of this picture book and discuss it as "Stage I." As a chronological unit the time span of Stage I is poorly defined. A rough radiocarbon estimate—and here we might as well bow to technology—would put it between 1200 and 500 B.C. There may have been some overlap from Stage I into Stage II. An orthodox remnant of Stage I ceremonial chiefs may have functioned south of the great pyramid while two or three generations of religious reformers developed Stage II. Before I undertake to outline my "stages," I would like to say that "stage" is not necessarily the word I like. I use it only to avoid confusion

Fig. 7.—La Venta: Monument "A." *(Photo by Stirling, after* CUCARF 5, 1968)

with what archaeologists have already outlined as "four phases." How my stages and periods correspond to their phases is an issue which can be debated later.

In Stage I, because of the aforementioned general lack of delimiting information, shall be included the great pyramid and its large platforms, as well as all the structures of Complex B and of the remainder of the island. With the already mentioned exception of the Stirling Acropolis, the structures in Complexes B and C are spaced and outlined with compatible grandiose ratios and proportions. Over most or perhaps over the entire time span of La Venta Stage I, the great pyramid was the focal point of religious orientation, I postulate for it a gradual growth by successive layers, one layer for each ceremonial chief buried there. If this hypothesis should some day be proven correct, then the height of the great pyramid would signify cultural stability probably for the entire time span of Stage I. A later portion of this study will attempt a rough definition of Stage I religion by approaching it as the "Age of Basalt."

With the beginning of Period I, Stage II, growth of the great pyramid ceased. The change may have begun innocently enough with the addition of a small platform at the north side of the pyramid. Then, northward on each side of a central axis, two long mounds were built. Later, in the northern half of the court, between these long mounds, a platform (A–3) was added for the burial of the first ceremonial chief outside the great pyramid. Presumably a new large pyramid could have risen there in time. But the accomplished break in tradition, from a vertical burial sequence to a place near the ground 470 feet farther north, was accompanied by an outburst of individualism which cannot be explained with only a change of burial sites. Tremendous amounts of creative energy were released, and construction moved northward and intensified at a steadily increasing rate. The burial mound of the Period I chief did not receive the body of a second leader; instead, the next leader pushed northward. An attempt will be made in a later section of this book to interpret these happenings as "Green Reform."

Period II in Stage II is a direct continuation of Period I. The underground "mosaic mask" of the previous stage was here developed into two massive "underground mosaic sculptures." These two mosaic sculptures, expressions of religious devotion literally "in depth," were capped with small platforms. The number of "two platforms" corresponds adequately to the two long mounds of the previous period. Consequently, the South Central Platform would have completed this chief's cycle of three structures. He could have been buried in his central platform. But no remains of him have been found at the center of this platform. I am therefore inclined to believe that this leader, in the prime of his life and at the peak of general religious enthusiasm, completed another cycle of construction before his death. The basalt column enclosure supports the interpretation that Periods II and III belong somehow together. The religious enthusiasm of these periods will be discussed later in relation to the "underground serpent sculptures."

Period III, possibly under the same leadership as the previous period, begins again with two small side platforms. These seem to have been put there primarily to satisfy tradition. Then, from the southern base lines of these side platforms, the designer swung the length of the base line northward to the center line to form an equilateral triangle. At this point of intersection, at the center of Mound A–2, the leader was to be buried when his time came. Before his time of death, however, he managed to supervise the largest underground mosaic sculptures in the history of the entire world. A description and interpretation will be given below.

The end of this period of religious enthusiasm and depth sculpturing is shrouded in a veil of incomplete data. The beginning of Period IV, therefore, is also uncertain. As a general characteristic of both Periods II and III of Stage II there should be noted the great emphasis which was put on getting deep into the earth. This signifies a clear reversal in the direction of religious devotion from the time of the great pyramid builders.

Period IV begins either with the second or with the third chief buried in Mound A–2. Concerning the second chief buried there we have insufficient information, but we know that the last two chiefs in Mound A–2 definitely belonged to a new historical period. Both show obvious traces of a Stage I orthodox backlash and a decline of the preceding depth-oriented pietism. Apart from their parasitic basalt-column tomb in the northern half of Mound A–2, and the enlargement of that mound which their burial required, they have left us no signs of construction. Instead, basalt sculpturing after the fashion of Stela 3 (Fig. 23, #28) was reintroduced. Their religious symbolism bears testimony to a syncretism between Stage I orthodoxy and Green Reform elements. Because this orthodox backlash is evident, it is possible that some Stage I religious practices might have been continued by a remnant group south of the great pyramid while the Green Reform has been flourishing to the north of it. However that may be, the ceremonial policies of the "Tomb A" chiefs backfired, and for the burial of the last of them only a few workmen were present to do the job. He was squeezed into a corner of his predecessor's tomb. His burial marks the end of Stage II, Period IV. Ceremonial activity north of the great pyramid ceased. And that moment in time, perhaps between 400 and 300 B.C., approximates the end of Olmec religious life at La Venta. A more detailed discussion of leaders, tombs, and the La Venta religious society will follow.

This historiographic sketch is in no way intended as a final solution to all Olmec problems. Michael Coe (1970) has succeeded in obtaining a reasonable chronology from refuse strata at the San Lorenzo site. Some day, when more information about San Lorenzo monuments and ceremonial structures has become available, a coordination with La Venta data can be attempted. Until now the greatest number of religiously relevant discoveries has come from La Venta. This is my reason for having wrestled with La Venta historiography. Our knowledge of Olmec religion is still too much dependent on the La Venta evidence. Some day, I trust, a broader synthesis will be possible.

4. The Center Line

The La Venta ceremonial center is oriented along a central axis, which registers on the compass eight degrees west of true north. In the combined report by Drucker, Heizer, and Squier (1959, p. 260) the view is expressed that with only minor modifications a basic master plan was adhered to from Phases I through IV—from about 1150 to 350 B.C. I started to explain my disagreement with this view above. At this point in the discussion, the reasons which underlie the interpretation which I rejected must be weighed more carefully. Basic for assuming an ever-present master plan for eight hundred years of La Venta construction is the presence of the center line.

Confronted with the fact that the line runs exactly eight degrees west of true north, not more and not less, the archaeologists (Drucker, Heizer, and Squier, 1959, p. 4) were justified in wondering about its possible meaning: "The northerly orientation may be pure chance or accident and may have been determined by the alignment of the natural clay and sand ridge upon which it is built"—or—this orientation may represent "a perpendicular to an east-west orientation obtained by observation of the rising or setting sun on a particular day in the Olmec calendar"—or—"some fixed star in the first half of the first millennium B.C. which then occupied the approximate position of Polaris today may have been the point of alignment."

There comes to mind the tremendous success which Gerald Hawkins had with decoding the astronomical portion of Stonehenge. Could a similar feat be accomplished at La Venta? The predictable has happened. In 1971 Marion P. Hatch published his "Hypothesis on Olmec Astronomy, with Special Reference to the La Venta Site." He has discovered something along the line which archaeologists have suspected. Not in the first half of the first millennium B.C., as was first anticipated, but around the year 2000 B.C. a significant astronomical phenomenon appeared in the direction eight degrees west of true north. At midnight of the summer solstice the "setting azimuth of C P Ursae Majoris" touched the northern horizon at the appropriate point (Hatch, 1971, p. 10). Hatch did not stop with his astronomical discovery but searched for additional support in the form of astral symbolism in Olmec iconography. He found similarities between the mouth of the jaguar and the outline of the Big Dipper. Moreover, he discovered that the historical Nahua name of the jaguar is identical with the name given to Ursa Major, namely, Ocelotl. Then, the approximate sign of Cynus, an "X", could be found engraved on four Olmec statues.

These astronomical investigations have gone a long way toward proving the original hypothesis. Nevertheless, it seems to me still that this entire effort was misdirected. Whatever the astronomical associations of the La Venta site might have been in late Olmec times, I remain convinced that stars do not explain the La Venta alignment. The ancient Olmecs were too

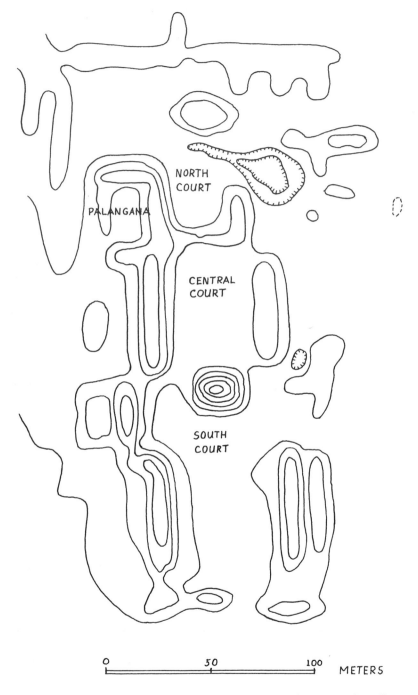

NORTH
COURT

PALANGANA

CENTRAL
COURT

SOUTH
COURT

0   50   100
METERS

Fig. 8.—Map of San Lorenzo Central Group. *(Drawn after Coe, 1967)*

38

much concerned with burrowing in the earth. Their celestial fascinations appear to have been at a minimum. I believe that the La Venta alignment can be explained much better in terms of natural topography. And Olmec topography, by the way, is not as accidental as it may seem to modern minds. Ridges to the Olmec people were not mere accumulations of dirt. From a world-wide comparative perspective I feel compelled to add a postscript for the benefit of future astronomical inquiries: While the astronomical aspects of Stonehenge have been brilliantly decoded, that megalithic site, too, meant certainly much more to its builders than a prefiguration of modern optical instruments. No human culture must be reduced to the narrow selections which later cultures develop.

A striking similarity exists between the layout of La Venta and the recorded topography of the central San Lorenzo site (Fig. 8). While the ground plans of the San Lorenzo and the La Venta central sites show an orientation on either side along center lines, it is even more remarkable that at both these major Olmec sites the general direction of orientation of the central complexes is north and south. Moreover, many post-Olmec ceremonial sites of Middle America were built by north and south alignments. These considerations are what made an astronomical explanation seem so plausible.

But it would certainly be a mistake to rest our conclusions on only two examples if more are available. Eight degrees west of true north at La Venta may have meant nothing to the original surveyors. Because, on the Northwest Ridge at San Lorenzo we find an alignment with an inclination east of true north by about the same number of degrees. Moreover, the Group C and D alignments at San Lorenzo run along a ridge from almost true west to east. Upon closer investigation we discover also that the central complex at San Lorenzo— that which has a north and south alignment— is oriented like its counterpart at La Venta along the main ridge of the area.

These observations clearly rule out the possibility of astronomical causality. At the same time I must admit that astronomical hypotheses are extremely difficult to disprove—they will always be so mathematically precise and appear so scientific. Moreover, there is bound to be present on some important day of the year, in some eligible millennium, and in every direction along any horizon some conspicuous star, constellation, or part of a constellation. I for my part have chosen to forgo this precision approach of investigation and instead concentrate on the over-all picture which is archaeologically given. The most conspicuous structural features at Olmec sites are mounds and ridges. With these I shall begin my interpretation of Olmec religious symbolism.

III

RIDGES AND VOLCANO HEADS

1. Pyramid on a Ridge

The most conspicuous feature at the La Venta site is its pyramid (Fig. 9). It stands 103 feet high, is located approximately at the center of the island, and has the shape of a fluted cone. Fanning out from the peak downward are ten ridges and gullies. Along the southern half of the pyramid these fans are spaced farther apart than at the north side. But the ground plan as a whole is still essentially symmetrical and oriented by the center line. Representing perhaps Middle America's oldest pyramid, this peculiar fanned mound naturally poses some questions.

Heizer and Drucker have advanced a long way toward solving the puzzle of the fluted pyramid (Heizer, Drucker, 1968, pp. 52 ff.). Michael Coe has narrated their discovery: The closest parallel to the form of the La Venta pyramid can be seen in the Tuxtla Mountains, the place from which the Olmecs had dragged their immense basalt boulders for their monuments. Dozens of small volcanic cones dot the region around beautiful Lake Catemaco in the center of the Tuxtlas. When Heizer was flying over this region one day the thought suddenly struck him—the La Venta pyramid is an imitation volcano! Exactly the same sort of ridges and gullies can be seen fanning out from each cone. Here was an example of architecture imitating nature. But, why should the Olmecs have done such a mad thing? Heizer had a suggestion. Assuming that the Olmec homeland was in the Tuxtla Mountains—since it is reasonable to assume that they knew basalt

Fig. 9.—La Venta: the pyramid, southeast view. *(Photo by Heizer, after CUCARF 8, 1970)*

working prior to coming to La Venta and prior to feeling the need for such materials—we surmise that they took "a little bit of home" with them to remind them of their volcano-surrounded origin point. Unfortunately, the Tuxtla volcanoes have meanwhile covered these possible homesites with cinders and lava—as late as two hundred years ago. Little hope exists that these suspected Olmec sites, perhaps a hundred feet below lava flows and cinders, will ever be found (Coe, 1968, p. 70f.).

The first interpretation, seeing an imitation volcano in the first among Middle America's pyramids, is probably correct. Nevertheless, the suggestion that people simply were desirous of "a little bit of home" and that these people therefore built an artificial mountain 103 feet high with imported materials, this, on the level of Stone Age technology, is inconceivable. A volcano to these people must have meant more than a memento or a geographical immensity. It is very likely that among the Olmecs a volcano signified nothing short of a cosmographic model.

Elsewhere in the world, volcanoes have impressed themselves on man as models for their cosmologies. The cosmology implied in Dante's *Divine Comedy*, for example, is based on this model. Purgatory extends upward along a cone, has purging fire at the top, and leads from there into heaven. Hell, as an inverted cone or "negative" volcano, contains the usual underworld reversals. Tartarus, in contrast to purgatory's flames, is a place of extreme cold.

So it would seem at least plausible that in the construction of an Olmec religious center a deeper religious motif had been present, namely, a response to the volcano as a greater-than-human configuration of reality. Fortunately, the La Venta artificial volcano is not altogether silent. This mountain has a face. While its eastern, its southern, and its western sides have only two ridges each, the northern slope has four. Thus, depending on what a volcano face in Olmec-land is supposed to look like, the mountain faces either north or south. North and south is the direction of the center line. Along that line must lie the meaning of the pyramid's directionality.

North of the artificial volcano, oriented along the center line, extends what archaeologists have designated "Complex A." In my earlier discussion of Olmec historiography, I introduced this area as constituting construction-stage two. Historical sequence was the main concern then; now I shall proceed with an analysis of the alignment itself. It has already been mentioned how the center line follows the main ridge of the island. From the pyramid northward this particular ridge is conspicuously visible for about two thousand feet. Immediately south of the pyramid that ridge comes to an end. Only farther south, on the other side of a depression, another natural ridge of similar size and proportions, continues southward in Complex B (Drucker, Heizer, and Squier, 1959, p. 8). Significant for our present concern is the end of the natural ridge just south of the volcano pyramid.

At this point I must give credit to a number of Southwest Indian sages and friends. On more than one occasion they have pointed to a long mountain range and explained to me what I was actually looking at. Big Snake lies there! Let me suppose, therefore, that the central ridge at La Venta was to the Olmecs a greater-than-human Serpent, then the artificial volcano on the end of that ridge, naturally, represents the Serpent's head. We have consequently two possibilities for interpreting the Serpent's position. Either the four ridges at the north slope of the mountain are his face, in which case the Serpent would have to be lying on his back; or, the north slope of the mountain represents the helmet scales on the Serpent's head and he lies in a normal prone position.[1] The latter alternative seems more natural. Thus, like the conspicuous helmets of the colossal basalt heads, which will be discussed later, so the differentiated north slope of the volcano represents the side opposite the Serpent's lower jaw. The mouth, I assume, points upward in volcano fashion.

There is additional support for the suggestion that La Venta's volcanic Earth Serpent faces south. He wears a bib. The platform, which corresponds proportionately to the size of the Serpent's head, faces southward to the area where structures of corresponding proportions are located. Complex B, or the Stage I ceremonial court, is situated directly in front of the great Serpent. The Earth Serpent's body faced south, and his people danced before him.

The religious significance of the La Venta pyramid has thus come into clearer light already. At the basis of Olmec religion lies the greater-than-human reality of the volcanic Earth Serpent. In the great mountain ranges of the Tuxtla area and in many other parts of the Middle American habitat gigantic serpents have raised their volcanic heads and have spread terror. So it would seem. And when the earth trembled, and when fire and smoke were blown from below into the atmosphere by an unseen monster, every human being was overcome with religious "awe." Fiery tongues of lava flowed from these volcanic mouths and split as they advanced. An Earth Serpent who can puff up a volcanic cone overnight, presumably, has unlimited power. His back is now where in earlier times his head used to be, and no one can tell where

---

[1]Professor Squier suggested in a conversation in June, 1974, that the ridges and gullies may have resulted from erosion subsequent to the abandonment of the site. Several such gullies are known to have formed along footpaths since 1955. The erosion history at the base of the pyramid has not been studied. Be that as it may, my interpretation of the central ridge and of the pyramid remains the same, regardless of ridges and gullies.

he will lift his head next. Modern man stands as helpless in his way as did the Olmecs of three thousand years ago. From this line of reasoning it would follow that a considerable portion of La Venta ceremonialism, in the terrible Serpent's path, had to do with placating this deity.

But fear and terror cannot have been the only responses of mortal Olmec builders. Nothing has ever been built by man without a measure of hope and positive fascination. Alluring visions from beyond the limits of what is known are essential for man to cross the thresholds of inherited traditions. This principle is as true in modern scientific pursuits as it was when the Olmecs arranged their ceremonial centers. Terror and fear alone discourage human creativity; they cause men to flee and, where flight is impossible, to attack and to destroy. In later centuries, at both La Venta and San Lorenzo, Olmec iconoclasts seem to have responded to traditional gods by attacking their representations—as atheists or reformers usually do. This phenomenon in Olmec culture will be discussed later. Presently it is necessary to follow a more difficult train of thought.

What aspect of the terrible volcanic Earth Serpent could possibly have inspired the Olmec people to become creative with architectural designs and with sculptures? What is there in a volcano that can inspire successive generations of maize planters to build artificial replicas of it? The answer cannot lie in the field of economics, nor with the alleged "human tendency for conspicuous waste of labor." Nor will an answer be forthcoming from Olmec sociology—as if a group has ever engaged in communal building projects primarily to survive as a group. Nothing drives a group of people apart faster than being obliged to work at an unreasonable project. No, the imitation of volcanic Serpent heads was essential to Olmec existence, essential in the most complete ontological sense. The answer to questions about the final motivation of Olmec builders lies along the religio-scientific dimension—in man's contact with greater-than-human reality configurations. As Christian groups to this day erect symbolic crosses in their sanctuaries, so the ancient Olmecs built Serpent heads to assure them of the immediacy of divine help and salvation. The numerous man-made long mounds and artificial ridges, which are present at several Olmec ceremonial centers, can be explained as Serpent bodies. Then, the Chalcatzingo evidence, which will be discussed next, is quite explicit about the Olmec rationale for constructing symbolic mounds.

2. The Chalcatzingo Relief

At a site near Chalcatzingo, at the foot of the Cerro de la Cantera, some sculptured basalt reliefs have been found. One of these bears directly on the religious meaning of the volcanic Earth Serpent (Fig. 10). I agree with Ignacio Bernal that these stone carvings might be late Olmec (Bernal, 1969, p. 138). The fact that they are late is not a hindrance, rather a help, for the present interpretation. As it happens in all religious systems, the original glimpse of reality diminishes as it is transmitted methodically or ceremonially from one generation to another. Consequently it becomes necessary for later icon makers and priests to express themselves more explicitly.

What we have in this relief is an ideogram of the Olmec agricultural world. The volcanic Earth Serpent is no longer facing upward but is adjusted to the horizontal dimension in accordance with the great Serpent's creeping incarnations—the specimens of herpetology. Great theistic visions often become reduced to the sizes and shapes of secondary avatars. Thus, whether the great Serpent's mouth faces upward or forward, it is still the mouth of the archaic volcanic Earth Serpent. The clouds which are depicted on this relief can signify both volcanic smoke and water vapors. To the maize planter in a volcanic territory both types of clouds mean the same thing—fertility and growth of his crops. It is well known, for instance, that after the last eruption of Sunset Crater in northern Arizona, Pueblo maize planters flocked to the area from far away to profit from the fertile ashes which had settled in the volcano's vicinity. Volcano-like clouds of smoke in slash-and-burn agriculture and rain clouds were also part of the Olmec world.

By relating these facts to the archaic maize planters, it is easy to see how the *mysterium tremendum* in the Olmec

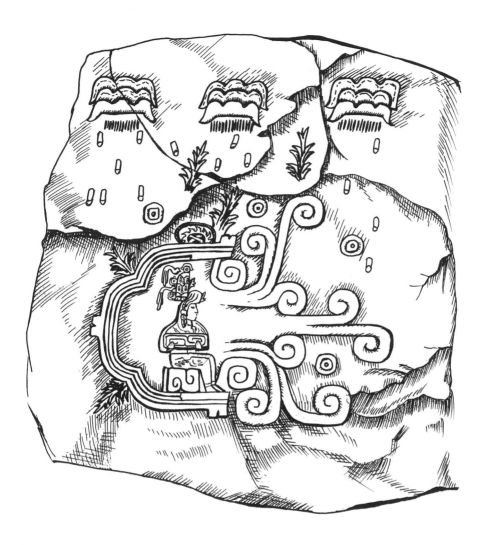

Fig. 10.—Chalcatzingo: Petroglyph 1. *(Drawn after Coe, 1968)*

experience could have become a *mysterium fascinans*. The volcano is a terrible, but also a productive force—it scares, but also fascinates and blesses. When it is not emitting fertile ashes it puffs up smoke. Smoke formations are the closest things to clouds, and the agency which can produce one thing is credited with producing the other. This line of reasoning still holds true today for smoking in Pueblo Indian rain ceremonies (i.e., Stephen, 1936, p. 306).

It is possible that the *mysterium tremendum* of Olmec religion has survived in a symbol at the top of the stylized Chalcatzingian mouth of the Earth Serpent. The volcano's fire symbol seems to be engraved there. However that may be, puffings from the great Serpent's mouth rise to form clouds; raindrops fall from these clouds to make maize grow from the Serpent's body. It is significant that these falling raindrops have phallic shapes, and phallic shapes—it must be obvious—resemble the anterior portions of snakes.

The person who sits in the mouth of the Chalcatzingo great Serpent can represent one of two personages—possibly both. He can represent the Serpent deity itself behind a humanoid mask, and, since he wears a snake-faced headgear he could also be a priest who has risen to the rank of an anthropomorphic divine mediator of the Earth Serpent's blessings. His headgear features the already familiar symbols of clouds and phallic raindrops.

It is significant that the Quetzal birds in the person's headgear are still portrayed as individual birds. They have entered the picture because their feathers are as green as the vegetation and because their tail feathers drape like the leaves of a maize plant and like serpent tails. At this stage of religious development the Quetzal birds have not yet visibly fused with the sacred snake person who wears them. This relief thus still antedates the birth of Quetzalcoatl, the famous Feathered Serpent of Middle America.

The phallic raindrops on the mediator's thigh are obvious, and so are the stylized serpent coils, similar to the great Serpent's puffings, which he holds at his breast and which he uses for his seat. A more elaborate discussion of snake persons will be called for below. The present explanations are intended to explain primarily the *mysterium fascinans* or the culture-inspiring aspect of the greater-than-human volcanic revelation. The Olmec people have shaped and carved symbolic Serpent heads because without the Earth Serpent's almighty presence, and without its manifold serpent manifestations, they could not have harvested and existed.

3. The Rain God's Paradise

The illustration introduced at this point is a mural from the Temple of Agriculture at Teotihuacán (Fig. 11). It dates from somewhere between A.D. 400 and 600. Since the time of its discovery it has generally been interpreted as depicting the paradise of Tlaloc. "Tlaloc" is the Aztec name of the rain god. He corresponds to the Maya "Chac," the Totonac "Tajin," and the Zapotec "Cocijo." What he was called in ancient times at Teotihuacán when the painting was created we do not know.

Different scholars have seen different things in "Tlaloc's Paradise." Walter Krickeberg, in his excellent summary of ancient Mexican cultures, saw it as a general abode of the dead (Krickeberg, 1956, p. 399). In it the departed spirits enjoy all the bliss and the pleasures of a paradise. "At the lower edge of the mural rises a mountain. At the foot of this mountain originate two rivers, marked with three-color stripes and lenticular water bubbles. These rivers meander in various directions and finally flow into lakes. Zapota and Cocoa trees, maize plants and various bushes, grow at the lake shores. A lively crowd of small people bustles about by the freshwater lakes."

Alfonso Caso, whose interpretation has inspired Krickeberg, elaborated more on this subject. Because I have been unable to find the original words of Caso, I must translate Krickeberg's German quotation (Krickeberg, 1956, pp. 399f.): "We note how roundabout the lake small and varicolored human figures bathe in the water and engage in other kinds of play. Some dive headfirst, others leap in with outstretched arms; one swims on his back, and another has left the water

and wrings his wrap-around towel. Water drops squeeze forth. At the bank of the river a few people rest under trees and pick flowers, while another chews at the stem of a maize plant. A little way up four people perform a strange dance whereby they follow each other, each reaching with one hand between his legs. The next person grasps the hand of his predecessor . . . . Here an adult carries a child on his back, and there four men try to chase a butterfly with branches in their hands. Almost all of these people speak or sing, and over the entire realm green jades lie scattered . . . . Only one individual seems not to participate in the joyousness around him . . . . While this man holds a green branch in his hand, heavy tears roll from his eyes. The symbol of speech from his mouth is five times repeated and indicates a lengthy chant—undoubtedly to the rain god. A symbol from the rain god's breast, con-

Fig. 11.—Teotihuacán: "Tlaloc's Paradise." *(Main portion at left, courtesy Museo Nacional de Antropología, Mexico. Extension at right, courtesy Peabody Museum, Harvard University)*

sisting of three shells entwined with a band, appears directly above the speech symbols."

Taken by themselves, with nothing but late Aztec mythology to illuminate the content of the Teotihuacán painting, the above interpretations represent indeed the work of masters. But the time has now come when we are no longer restricted to looking at Mesoamerican "mountains" backward through time. Knowing that an Olmec volcano was the Earth Serpent's head, we immediately recognize this head in the Teotihuacán fresco. The lower portion of this painting, taken by itself, is more orthodox Olmec than its forerunner, the Chalcatzingo relief. The Great Serpent's mouth, over a millennium later and about seventy miles farther north, is righted again to where it faces upward like a volcano. Now it does not seem any more as though the Teotihuacán mural depicts an other-worldly paradise of the rain god. Rather, this is Olmec cosmography made explicit.

The primary difference between the Chalcatzingo relief and the Teotihuacán painted volcano is that the anthropomorphic figure in the mouth of the former has in the latter joined his cloud products in the sky. The birds of his headgear have surrendered their individuality and merged into the immense feather hat of the cloud god; they have also given him a beak. The cloud symbol of the Chalcatzingo relief has nevertheless entered unchanged into the lower central body portion of the cloud god.

Most interpreters have separated, I think mistakenly, the upper portion of the mural from the lower and have seen the combination of the two portions as arbitrary. In this manner the upper half was separately interpreted as showing the rain god rising from the ocean (i.e., Krickeberg, 1956, p. 398). Taken as a whole, however, this mural shows neither an ocean nor a lake. The rain god, along with his helpers, is enthroned above a layer of clouds after the fashion of a towering cumulus cloud. This interpretation, then, leaves the lower portion of the mural as a simple vertical crosscut of the planters' real world.

The fact that the upper world of the cloud–rain god is separated from the planter world by a distinct layer of serpentlike designs need not disturb us. From the point of view of earth surface people a cloud layer always separates the surface realm from the invisible world above the clouds. People who are familiar with Mexican mountain and coastal weather have attested to the occurrence of thick cloud layers and spectacular cumulus clouds.

The cumulus-cloud–rain god in the upper world has in Teotihuacán become the celestial parallel of the volcanic head of the Earth Serpent which in the painting is situated immediately below. The mediator has risen to a place above the clouds. His ascent has been helped by his association with bird symbolism—by feathers and beak. Moreover, this separation of the Cloud Serpent from the Earth Serpent has been prepared for by late Olmec priests who, after the fashion of the Chalcatzingo relief (Fig. 10), have added birds to their headgear. This development marks the end of traditional Olmec earth-orientedness and demonstrates the gradual birth of a feathered Serpent. The Aztecs knew this deity as Quetzalcoatl. From Olmec to Aztec the history of Middle American civilization can be seen as a span of time in which the Earth Serpent, in the form of one of his manifestations, has learned to fly.

In the maize planter world, depicted in the lower half of the Teotihuacán mural, many of the small figures do indeed represent spirits of the departed. A link with similar spirit figures on La Venta Stelae 2 and 3 seems almost certain. In any case, the open mouth of the volcano is an entrance into which some are going and from which many more are emerging and have already emerged. Who can, at the sight of this scene, keep from being reminded of the Pueblo Indian kachinas? The kachina divinities, too, are related to clouds and rain, and to success in maize growing. Frequently they are also thought of as the spirits of the dead. Significantly, Hopi kachinas in late summer return to the San Francisco Peaks—the largest volcanic crater in northern Arizona. One kachina lives in Sunset Crater, a cinder cone, near by.

A number of sacred mountains near Pueblo villages have mouths at their summits which need to be fed. Whether there is a shrine on the eastern mountain of the Hopi world (Mount Taylor) is uncertain; but the mouth of Mount Baldy (south) receives turquoise and shell offerings. There is talk about a shrine on the San Francisco Peaks (west); and Navajo Mountain (north) has on its south side a shallow sacred cave with a spring in it. In a similar fashion, the four sacred mountains of the San Juan Tewa world—Truchas Peak (east), Sandia Crest (south), Tsikomo Mountain (west), Conjilon Peak (north)—feature on their tops a "navel." Inside these navels live the Towa-é who led the people during their emergence from the underworlds; from their respective mountain tops they watch over the Tewa world. The next inner circle in Tewa geography consists of four flat-topped hills, *tsin*, which are said to have been created by the Towa-é of the four larger mountains. These smaller sacred hills correspond thus ideologically to the man-made ceremonial pyramids of Middle America. Each *tsin* has a cave and/or tunnels running through it. All are believed inhabited by Tsave Yoh, a group of supervisory whipping kachinas. People have been captured and taken inside by them. A Tsave Yoh would periodically capture children and feed them to his family (Ortiz, 1969, pp. 19, 142). Such mythic memories clearly link these Tewa hills with the hungry pyramidal Serpent mouths of Middle America and the role of the Tsave Yoh with the roles of Middle American sacrificial priests. Moreover, the Tewa memory goes back even to the Olmec volcanic era: two of these Tewa *tsin* are places from which smoke and fire are said to have belched forth in ancient time.

On the multidimensional body of the Earth Serpent in the Teotihuacán mural grow the plants which are necessary for human survival. The people who are shown on the surface are mortals tending these plants. The Serpent's multiple bodies or ridges terminate with secondary heads. The one which can be seen in cross section on the far right would appear from the surface as a mound. On that mound a priest with tearful eyes sings his chant and waves his branch. Tears, chant, and branch are all indications of his wish to the god. The rain god, as Cloud Serpent, answers with living water from above. In addition to what has already been said by others, I would like to add my suggestion with regard to the "speech curls." All these curls are double. They are split like the tongues of snakes, split also after the fashion of maize plants after they have pierced the ground.

Fig. 12.—Teotihuacán: Chalchiuhtlicue, the water goddess. (Courtesy Museo Nacional de Antropología, Mexico)

Fig. 13.—Teotihuacán: Xipe Totec, Our Lord the Flayed One.
(Courtesy Museo Nacional de Antropología, Mexico)

The more complete meaning of the Teotihuacán painting will emerge later in the light of the discussion of Olmec tombs, figurines, and Snake people. The present intention has been to demonstrate the continued presence of the Olmec volcanic Earth Serpent in the history of Middle American religions. Alfonso Caso tells that the Aztecs gave the name of the rain god, Tlaloc, to a mountain range (Caso, 1958, pp. 42, 60). The Aztecs also believed that the realm of the rain god was located to the south. It was thought of as a fertile place where all kinds of fruit trees grew, where maize, beans, and other foodstuffs abounded. Sahagún, in his brief reference to the Olmecs, even identified the original realm of the rain god with the Olmec homeland (Dibble & Anderson, Bk. 10, pp. 187 f.). It seems therefore very likely that early models of the rain god's lower realm, in the Teotihuacán mural, are the Olmec religious centers of San Lorenzo and La Venta.

The divine offspring of the Olmec Earth Serpent can be found elsewhere among the monuments of Teotihuacán. Below, with Figure 16, I shall have an occasion to introduce the so-called pyramid of Quetzalcoatl which features rattlesnake reliefs all over. But even the famous statue of the Water Goddess, Chalchiuhtlicue (Fig. 12), which has been found in the plaza below the so-called "Pyramid of the Moon," represents a snake deity. Not only is she still remembered as the Lady of the Jade Skirts (and therefore "serpentine"—see below), she shows on her skirt an explicit diamondback serpent pattern. A serpentlike band hangs across her arms. But, still more convincingly, she has large Olmec earrings and a cleft at the center of her headgear.

The Teotihuacán Xipe Totec (Fig. 13) is likewise a serpent deity. His belt is a snakeskin. His loose headskin has fallen to the neck and is folded inside out. Snakes to this very day are accustomed to shed their skins in exactly this manner. The general association of Xipe Totec with young maize and with spring harmonizes well with this manner of serpentine rejuvenation. The husking of ears of maize may have come to be symbolically associated with the serpent's shedding of its skin. It is also possible that human penes and foreskins have been associated with the Xipe Totec figure. No rationale,

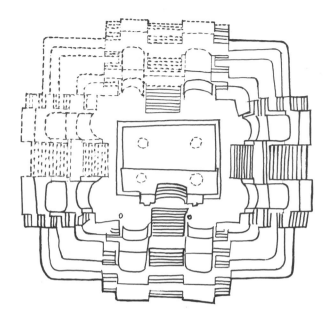

Fig. 14.—Uaxactún: Structure E–VII. *(Drawn after Bernal, 1969)*

aside from the associated rejuvenation of serpents by shedding their skins from the head backward, explains the widespread practice of circumcision better. Moreover, quite in line with straight logical progression, a serpent-maize-man mysticism of this kind will eventually demand that human victims be flayed. Men in all cultures imitate and try to become what they have envisioned as exemplary greater-than-human manifestations of reality.

4. Serpent Heads and Coils

In ancient Middle American culture it would be a mistake to separate architecture from sculpture. Clay models from Aztec times still bear witness to this fact (i.e., Pollock, 1936). Were it not for the presence of steps on one of these pyramid models, it could be mistaken for an Olmec statuette of the phallic pillar type which has faces protruding from its side. In like manner, when Olmec builders heaped their mounds on ridges they sculptured heads of their great Earth Serpent. When later architects elaborated on the simple mounds, they were still modeling the features of divine Serpents.

There is more to be said about the subsequent architectural history of the Olmec artificial volcano. Serpent heads were constructed in Middle America up to the time when the symbol of the serpent bruiser of Genesis 3:15—the cross of Christ—usurped their central place. A few examples shall suffice here to illustrate the continued presence of the Olmec Serpent in Middle America.

The ground plan of the La Venta fluted cone, if one discounts the specially arranged north slope and considers the paired ridges on each of the three remaining sides, can easily be recognized again in the Uaxactún pyramid, Structure E–VII (Fig. 14). This pyramid dates from about A.D. 325 and has been classified as "formative Mayan." It could also be called "post-Olmecian." A similar ground plan can be found a few miles south from there at Tikal. The hundred-foot-high "preclassic" pyramid, Structure 5–C–54, stretches upward from a fluted base.

The typical pyramid in Maya-land stretches high to reach above the deep tropical forest. Long, steep stairways lead directly into the open mouths of these pyramidal serpents. The interior of the mouth of some of them is divided into three successive chambers, which seems to indicate that distinctions were made with regard to certain degrees of being swallowed. The ultimate state of being swallowed, as happens to be the case with complete surrender in every religion, meant the death of the individual. Whether this state of ultimate religious surrender refers to the high priest's burial in the center of the pyramid, or whether a person died the routine death of regular sacrificial victims, their state of religious surrender was ultimate. At the same time one can be reasonably sure that those who were previously initiated into the secrets of the cult knew how to take advantage of their fate even in death.

The visitor to Maya-land may notice that the modification of the La Venta volcano head has led there to a new kind of

Fig. 15.—Calixtlahuaca: Temple of Quetzalcoatl. *(Drawn after Marquina, 1964)*

Fig. 16.—Teotihuacán: Temple of Quetzalcoatl. *(Drawn after Marquina, 1964)*

architectural design. The Serpent has in the land of the Olmecs only lifted his head; among the Maya he stretched his neck above the trees of the jungle and grew taller. Elaborate stairways had to be built to enable the human daredevil priests to climb straight into the most sacred mouth. Stairs were also necessary to bridge the obvious coils of a Serpent who meanwhile had come out from the earth and positioned himself completely on the surface. Important consequences followed from this new arrangement. Serpents whose entire length lay coiled on the surface of the earth no longer required natural ridges to account for the presence of their bodies. The independent pyramid, itself, became a mediator between the earth and the world above the clouds. The Pyramid Serpents were entirely the work of men; their builders rose therefore to the rank of full-fledged creator gods—they had even become powerful creators of gods.

Round coils are indicated in the pyramids at Cuicuilco (ca. 300 B.C.), in the late so-called "Temple of Quetzalcoatl" at Calixtlahuaca (Fig. 15), and elsewhere. The ascent to the top of a number of Aztec pyramids requires circling them several times as if to follow the serpent coils to their heads. The famous "Pyramid of Quetzalcoatl" at Teotihuacán has been constructed specifically to assist the Mesoamerican religious memory—just in case the meaning of the pyramids should some day be forgotten (Fig. 16). On the entablatures of every pyramidal coil, for everyone to see, a relief design of the great Serpent encircles the structure. And especially for observers who habitually confuse serpent bodies with mere decorative "bands," the builders have added at regular intervals replicas of the Serpent's heads and of his rattles. No mistaking is possible now. The Pyramid Serpent is for real. And we can assume that it is one of those many emancipated Earth Serpents whose hungry mouths at the top of the structures have required feeding.

Walter Krickeberg is probably correct when he questions the relationship of this Teotihuacán pyramid with Quetzalcoatl, the "feathered" or "winged" Serpent (Krickeberg, 1956, p. 398). The presence in the design of shells and snails links this Pyramid Serpent with earth and water—not with the realm of feathers and wings. Too many Middle American Serpents have been called Quetzalcoatls. On that same Teoti-

Fig. 17.—Excerpt from *Codex Borgianus* (14) by Eduard Seler.
(Fondo de Cultura Económica, Mexico, 1963)

huacán ceremonial site rest other and far more gigantic Serpent coils. The so-called "Pyramid of the Sun" and the
"Pyramid of the Moon" are coiled Serpents as well. It just so
happened that a small and late structure at this immense
ceremonial center was supplied with more obvious serpentine
identification marks.

Quetzalcoatl, the feathered or winged Serpent, appears to
have been only one of the Great Serpent's manifestations.
The precise time of his appearance on the Middle American
scene will remain a subject for many years of research to
come. Together with his appearance the advent of the eagle
and the jaguar gods must also be studied. None of these seems
to have been very significant in the earliest stratum of Middle
American civilization. Coiled pyramidal Serpents, however,

can be traced to the Olmec mounds by means of which the Earth Serpent first lifted his head. It is possible that some day even more archaic mounds than the Olmecian will be found.

In case a critical reader should still doubt the "coiled serpent" interpretation of Middle American pyramids, I shall point to a late and therefore more explicit source. What pyramid tops still meant to a late Aztec or Mixtec author is shown unambiguously in Codex Borgia 14 (Fig. 17). The pyramidal superstructure, in side view, is very obviously an open mouth. Along this same line of reasoning it would seem that architectural pillars, at the front and along the forward portion of the sides of many pyramidal structures, indicate the fangs of the Serpent. What Codex Borgia 14 reveals pictorially about pyramid tops, a Malinalco temple tells in three dimensions (Fig. 49). The temple is a sculpture of the Serpent's mouth. More concerning the Serpent's mouth and Malinalco will be said in Chapter VI. Here we must recognize that architecture in Middle America, to the very last, has remained sculpture. It is to smaller sculptures that we must now turn.

IV

VOLCANIC SERPENT FACES

1. People in the Serpent's World

To understand Olmec religion, Olmec art and life, one must make an effort to see all things as belonging to a world different from ours. This was a world where mountain ranges and ridges were Serpent bodies, where hills and volcanoes were Serpent heads, and in which men built Serpent-head ceremonial centers for their serpentine world order to unfold round about.

When I first began looking at Middle American religion, I did not expect to find an ever-present Serpent. As a child of Mediterranean civilization, I searched first for evidence of a *magna mater*, a Great Mother Earth. According to Mother Earth theology, as for example in the Greek myth of Deucalion, stones in the earth are the bones of the Great Mother. In Middle America the few figurines of "fertility goddesses" are very unconvincing. Many of the female figurines there represent anything else but fertility. There had to be a more unified vision of reality; everything else in ancient Middle America points to a coherent ideology. This central vision and key to Middle American reality, since the time of the Olmecs, has been the great Serpent in his numerous manifestations.

Not only things and creatures which fascinate modern herpetologists belonged to the great Earth Serpent's world. The great mountain-range Serpent puffed serpent curls of smoke from his volcanic mouths; these smoke curls joined serpentine layers of clouds. From these clouds fell serpentine/

Fig. 18.—Young maize plants.

phallic raindrops which caused young maize plants to sprout
from the Earth Serpent's body. The green tips pierced the
soil and quickly split after the fashion of serpent tongues
(Figs. 18, 19). After having grown tall, the leaves of the maize
plant drooped like serpent tails (Fig. 20). In due time the
planters harvested and ate serpent fruit and serpent seeds.
The link between rattlesnakes and maize has been made very
explicit in the case of the Aztec Chicomolotzin (Fig. 21). Not
only are the scales of this serpent arranged like kernels on a
long corncob, the ears of maize themselves protrude like large
scales. *Der Mensch ist was er isst*—"man is what he eats"—
or, he gradually discovers that his essence must be explained
by the same story which explains the essence of his food. The
ultimate "ground of being" of maize planters is the maize that
sustains them. As Pueblo Indian planters well know, their
bodies consist of corn—of the flesh of sacrificial maize divini-

Fig. 19.—Split tongue of an anaconda.

ties. The Olmecs gave credit to the sacrificial maize/serpent divinities for their humanoid existence.

In the same line of reasoning about essentials, when an Olmec man contemplated his manhood, he understood his procreative endowments in terms of what they really looked like—serpentine shapes and powers. In this manner, apparently, the religion of the Great Serpent favors manhood and slights womanhood—at least our notion of womanhood.

Since all the Olmec ceremonial centers seem to have been the creations of men's associations, led by priestly chiefs, we do not really know what the personal religious life of the women was like. For all we know, they may have prayed to an earth mother. Nevertheless, this much is certain: in whatever home activity or agricultural task they cooperated with their menfolk, they acquiesced to the way of the Serpent. In our modern way of thinking—if we try to approximate Olmec

Fig. 20.—A Hopi maize field.

categories part way—women are people of the nonphallic/
serpentine kind. But such a classification is not sufficiently
Olmec yet. In the Olmec religious world women played an
integral and vital role; they are even represented in the sacred
Serpent sculptures. They were associated with the Serpent's
mouth. I am now convinced that the widespread American
Indian concept of the *vagina dentate* had its beginning in this
positive ideological context.

The manner of associating womanhood with the Serpent's
mouth was not at all intended to be derogatory. On the contrary. The Serpent's mouth, as we have seen already in Figure
17 and shall have occasion to see again in Chapter VI, was
considered to be the most sacred place on earth. Where, and

Fig. 21.—The Aztec Chicomolotzin. *(Courtesy Museo Nacional de Antropología, Mexico)*

in what particular form or measure, the serpentine mouth has been revealed in a given instance was of secondary importance. In accordance with the great Serpent's way and will, all Snake people had their holes. Small snakes had small crevice entrances to the body of the Earth Serpent; serpentine planter folk lived in pit houses; and, adult Snake men had their women. The Serpent's mouth was a place of refuge, the creative womb from which all things were born and to which all things returned. The fact that this sacred place appears in actual life often guarded by rows of dangerous teeth was not the Olmecs' fault. These people simply recognized what we so often overlook—that eating and biting precedes growth as much as impregnation precedes birth.

2. The Age of Basalt

In the study of a religion it would be far more appropriate to name a historical epoch after a divine power which reigned over it. Unfortunately, in an attempt at reconstructing a prehistoric religion this is not always possible. In the absence of spoken and written words we are forced to draw our categories from the second clearest layer of religious expression—physical iconography. Along with mounds and ridges, the Olmec sites of Stage I contain primarily basalt carvings and statues. The considerable distance of approximately sixty miles, over which basalt blocks had to be transported, while other kinds of stone would have been much nearer at hand, indicates that the basalt material itself had some religious significance (Fig. 22).

The modern archaeologist, being always appreciative of durable cultural evidences, is inclined to suspect in the choice of basalt an effort on the part of the Olmec creators to score in twentieth century historiography and archaeological records. It need not be ruled out categorically that the idea of making memorials for the benefit of future generations may have affected the Olmec ambitions of building civilization. Nevertheless, I happen to be convinced that the durability of Olmec art works is a by-product and was not the primary motivating factor for selecting raw materials.

In the beginning of the Olmec world was the great Earth Serpent—or several Serpent manifestations. The Earth Serpent raised his volcanic heads, and from the open mouths at the top of these volcanic heads rose smoke. Fiery streams of lava flowed from these mouths and split.[1] Clouds formed above their craters and calderas. In thin serpentine streaks fell the rain, and, uniting with greater snakelike rivulets, the rushing waters gradually washed heaps of volcanic ash and cinders down and outward on the alluvial fans. In the course of many millennia the rocky cores of ancient volcanoes were washed bare. Huge basalt boulders, the remains of massive lava flows, could then be found strewn over the countryside.

---

[1] I am now convinced that all the fiery dragons in the mythologies of the world have as their ontological basis the hierophany of the volcanic Earth Serpent.

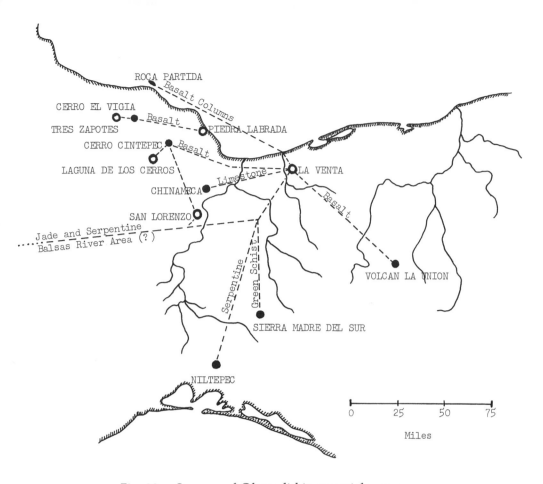

Fig. 22.—Sources of Olmec lithic materials, map.

Many of them occurred in their natural shapes as spheres.

When many ages later the earliest of the Olmecs appeared on the scene, having recently become interested in agriculture and in things pertaining to the soil, they could not but wonder about these roundish "heads." Spherical and in the shape of heads, whose heads were they? When recently Matthew Stirling from the Smithsonian Institution did report about the occurrence of such natural basalt spheres in Mexico, he explained their origin in association with lava flows (Stirling, 1969, pp. 294 ff.). The early Olmecs did the same. Lava flows and blackish stones, they knew from experience, were born from the volcanic mouths of the Great Serpent. Small heads, logically, were children of the large one. In assuming thus for the Olmecs what has already been established in the previous chapter, a greater-than-human volcano and mountain-range revelation, volcanic boulders would naturally have been encountered as important manifestations of that same reality configuration.

When sacred objects are first discovered in their religious context, they are simply revered. Prayers might be addressed to them as to divine persons and mediators of blessings; gifts might be deposited before them. Had the Olmec people preserved that pure and pristine religious attitude toward their sacred boulders, we would now see these same boulders without ever knowing anything about the people who three thousand years ago were fascinated by them. But, as it happened with other peoples of the world, so also the Olmecs scored in history because their war on greater-than-human realities, their quest for civilization, has left for posterity an admirable heap of archaeological evidence—broken armory from their battles with the gods.

Civilization is a process begun by human culture heroes who, in their struggle against traditional greater-than-human reality configurations, have dared to modify the faces of these configurations. In the process of redefining them they have managed to reduce some of them to less-than-human and controllable entities. In the new freedom of action which the hero discovers through his daring experiments, he manipulates his newly identified less-than-human realities while the masses of people still stand in awe. Thus the mediator between the people and the sources of power becomes awe-inspiring himself. The masses of people are thus challenged to trust their culture hero—priest, artist, scientist, conqueror, or other—and to accept his revised definitions of human possibilities and limitations. The result is civilization, measurable in terms of human creativity and mass production.

Culture heroes are already known from early hunter societies. Like the culture heroes of all society types, they come in at least two sizes. There is the ideal hero of mythology whose success is a matter of record; then there are his numerous incarnations, shamans, and charismatic leaders. In hunter myths the ideal culture heroes appear as archetypal shamanic tricksters, who gave to the world of hunters its form, its purpose, as well as the necessary means and skills for the continuance of hunting. The culture heroes of hunters are tricksters because trickery is the primary technique in hunting. As were his colleagues of subsequent ages, the culture hero of hunters was faced with an overwhelming measure of greater-than-human reality configurations. For him these were mostly the lords or divine owners of animals; but he also had to contend with offended spirits of animals and their spirit guardians whom the hunters had violated in their pursuit of meat. In this type of a world the culture hero is required to be an expert in tricking animals as well as in tricking the gods who own the animals; once the anger of divinities is aroused he must also know how to placate them. Thus, for his personal safety he needs a strong guardian spirit who will defend his cause and the cause of his fellow hunters against all other greater-than-human odds.

When hunters became planters, the basic problem of remaining on workable terms with greater-than-human powers remained the same. But there came a difference. To people whose attention was given primarily to the earth, greater-than-human reality configurations appeared from that direction. The hero of agriculture—as a mythical or an incarnate personage—was no longer called upon to mediate or to spearhead man's aggressive impact on the animal world; rather, he was now a mediator to the powers of earth and vegetational growth. Like his predecessor, the trickster shaman of the hunters, the agriculturist hero tried his hand at modifying the will of his gods. Gradually, the persistent modification of divine wills changed the human understanding of the gods themselves; it changed also the profiles of those who directly dealt with the gods.

Changes of divine faces in Olmec history were preceded by the willful change of their locations. The first Olmec culture hero is a nameless planter, perhaps a courageous survivor of the earlier order of hunter shamans. He took one of these sacred basalt heads, Serpent power, and placed it in his maize field. As a result of his daring deed he had stationed in his own little realm and for his own particular needs a divine ambassador of the great Earth Serpent. For many generations, perhaps, this type of divine representative might have been

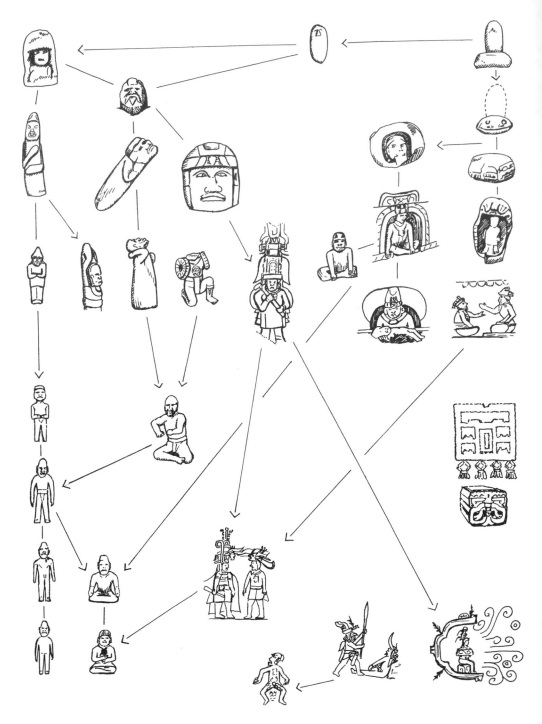

Fig. 23.—Olmec sculpture sequences.

STAGE I

#11
La Venta
Monument "A"

#10
Cerro d.l.Mesas
Stela 1

#1
Izapa
Stela 13
Altar 9

#12
Tonala
Monument 5

#2
Izapa
Altar 2

#13
From
Huame-
lulpan

#6
La Venta
Altar 7

#14
Tres
Zapotes
Mon. F

#15
La Venta
Monument 1

#3
Izapa
Altar 1

#7
La Venta
Altar 4

#4
Izapa
Monument 2

#17
La Venta
Mon.12

#19
S.Lorenzo
Mon.34

#8
La Venta
(1905)

#16
La Venta
(south)

#18
From
La Venta

#20
La Venta
Stela 2

#9
La Venta
Altar 5

#5
La Venta
Altar 3
west side

STAGE II

#21
La Venta
Tomb C
Green Reformer

#22
Santa Maria Uxpanapa
Wrestler

#24
La Venta
Mosaic-
Sculpture

#23
La Venta
Tomb B
Successor I

#25
La Venta
Tomb B
Sarcophagus

(Successor II missing)

#28
La Venta
Stela 3

#26
La Venta
Tomb A
Successor III

#27
La Venta, Tomb A
Successor IV

#30
Monte Alban
Danzante Figure

#29
Chalcatzingo Relief

revered devoutly by everyone in the household or village. But one bit of human knowledge—experimental knowledge—this lithic Serpent representative would never live down; he had been placed according to the desire and will of a human hero. Gradually the human role in the world of serpents became ritualized: controls from the dimension of space could by way of ritualization be extended into the dimension of time.

This line of reasoning leads me to date the unhewn Izapa-type altars and stelae earlier than the modified versions of La Venta, San Lorenzo, and other places. My diagram of Olmec sculpture sequences, Figure 23, is presented only as an approximation of what might have been the sequential development. It is based on an imcomplete list of Olmec monuments, and in no way should it be used for identifying specific monuments as prototypes of specific later specimens. The small jade and serpentine figurines of Stage II, coming as they do from specific burials of successive generations, are an exception rather than the rule with regard to the specificity of this diagram.

Pairs of stones, consisting of an upright pillar and a flat slab of the Izapa type, have been found in many parts of the world. Many speculations about their original significance have been made. It is questionable whether similar arrangements everywhere in the world meant the same thing. Judging from the Izapa development and elucidation in Monument 2, I personally believe that the upright and the flat stones together signify male and female entities. Concerning some upright stones of western Europe, menhirs, it is known that some of them were visited till recent times by womenfolk. Some are called "sliding stones," and sliding from them would help a woman conceive. Concerning other menhirs in Europe it is still being said that if one listens closely, one will hear babies cry inside. These instances point to the broad religious involvement of stones in man's concern for fertility. I do not suspect from this parallel that megaliths were associated as intensely with serpents in Europe as they were in Middle America. The basic association of upright stones with phalli, or their significance as bones, i.e., life-concentrations of Mother Earth, is sufficient to explain their placement. In addi-

Fig. 24.—Monte Alto: Monument 4. *(Photo by Parsons, after* CUCARF *11, 1971)*

tion to their phallic meaning, the megaliths of Middle America have obtained an extra significance as offspring of the volcanic Earth Serpent; as such they captured the planters' imagination and their entire concern for fertility and growth. After all, serpents may be only emancipated phalli.

From changing the locale of a snake god to redefining his character is only a small step. In fact, the latter is an inescapable consequence. By yielding his former place to accommodate the wishes of men, the lithic Serpent representative showed his man-friendly nature. He deserved a more personal face than he originally had. Apparently, the earliest engravings were not intended as alterations at all. They were simply attempts to outline that which was already present in obscure form (i.e., Fig. 23, No. 2, 12, and Fig. 24). This is essentially the same religious attitude with which Michelangelo approached his blocks of Italian marble. But even a devout sculptor changes the appearance of his stone, and with it he redefines its nature for other observers. Worshipers of gods eventually become their controlers; religion becomes science.

Some early Olmec sculptures resemble phalli very closely. But phalli by themselves still have no faces. At the same time, protruding basalt heads, as they were found on the slopes of volcanoes, were similar to other protruding heads. Heads of serpents, which were protruding from below boulders and bushes, suggested most of the facial expressions which their lithic brothers were given to wear. Judging from the Izapa and La Venta sequences in Figure 23, it seems that both female and male stones have obtained their initial faces in that manner. But then, as the sculptor-priest began triumphing over serpent substances, his human face soon competed with the snake faces for representation in stone. Anthropomorphic faces gradually emerged more clearly from the mixture. This change reflects on the one hand the sculptor-priest's changing concept of himself, his increasing closeness to deity, and on the other it illustrates man's success at redefining serpentine reality. Anthropomorphic visions of greater-than-human reality, in the end, will always prevail; they are the most inclusive symbols by which man can grasp the meaning of his human existence. If the basis of our existence is not personal, what does it mean to be human?

Among the more peculiar elements of Olmec sculpture are what appear to be helmets. La Venta Monument A seems to suggest a phallic shape as prototype for the Olmec helmets. Most of the later evidence, however, leans more toward serpent prototypes. In past scholarly interpretations of Olmec heads, jaguars could never be made to rhyme with Olmec helmets. The world has yet to breed its first helmeted jaguar. Football helmets from the world of men have been suggested as a possibility. The problem is more easily solved if snakes are being considered as prototypes. Many snakes have heavy head scales, the component portions of which are still evident in the stylized helmet patterns of some colossal Olmec heads. In any case, the outlines of these helmet patterns resemble snake head scales much closer than they do jaguar spots (Figs. 25, 26, 23, No. 15).

Fig. 25.—La Venta: Monument 4. *(Courtesy Smithsonian Institution)*

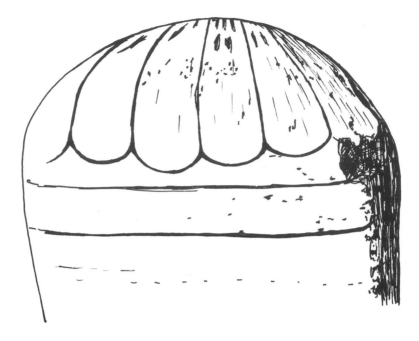

Fig. 26.—La Venta: Monument 4, rear view. *(Drawn after Stirling, 1943)*

A world of surprises may lie in store for the researcher who will compare Olmec helmet patterns with living specimens of Mexican snakes. Two thousand miles away from Olmec-land I try to reconstruct an ancient world view with only an incomplete set of photographs at my disposal. Try as I may, bending the photo prints will not give me the necessary top views of the heads. Only one good rear view of a La Venta colossal head has been published, and that pattern points to a design which I remember having seen on the head of an African green colubrid constrictor. I have not been able to see the Mexican representatives of that snake family. But if this hint should ever lead to something, I reckon, it would be significant to note that colubridae are snake-eating snakes. Could it be that these snakes, specifically, were thought of as incarnations of the rain god who later among the Aztecs became known as Tlaloc? Sahagun's Nahuatl text of an Aztec snake ceremony may be somehow related to such snake-eating snakes. Seler and Fewkes have come up with the following translation:

> The statue of Tlaloc was placed before the water in which snakes and frogs were, and the so-called Macateca (a people who lived east of the road to Oaxaca) swallowed the snakes and frogs alive, one by one. They seized them only with the mouth and not with the hand; with the teeth only they grasped them when they seized them in the water before the statue of Tlaloc; and while the Macateca were trying to swallow the snakes, they performed a dance, and he who had first swallowed a snake began to cry "papa papa" and danced around the temple, and they rewarded those who had swallowed the snakes. (Fewkes, 1893, p. 290.)

The use of frogs in these ceremonies sheds new light on a few froglike statues in the Olmec repertoire. Frogs and snakes are both linked with water and rain. What kind of snakes were being swallowed or held between the teeth by the dancers we do not know. But we do know that today some Hopi men still dance with mostly rattlesnakes between their teeth. Prior to their dancing, in the kiva, these snakes are also given a bath. After their ceremonial dancing the men vomit in unison. More about Hopi practices will be said in Chapter VII. By comparison, the next chapter will show that the rattlesnake definitely played an important role in the Olmec ceremonial life during Stage II.

A shortage of Mexican snakes in my part of the world is a serious handicap for this interpretative study. The usual representations of snakes in herpetology textbooks are not of much help. Rarely do they show the body portion which on the basis of sculptures one suspects to be relevant. Most scarce of all are full-face "personal" portraits of snakes; they are, as I now know well from experience, very difficult to make. Their scarcity, nevertheless, seems to be more the result of Western man's general dislike for serpent faces. This much can be said: The cumulative evidence of what lately I have seen of snakes, far outweighs anything which can be said in favor of a jaguar ancestry for Olmec helmets.

The faces of Olmec statues themselves are even more convincing. The famous drooping mouth and snarling lips I interpret as being definitely serpentine. True, a jaguar can snarl and look mean; but the one important thing which he will never do is to get rid of his hourglass-shaped feline nose. The typical nose of an Olmec statue is flat, triangular, and has a horizontal base line. Jaguar noses are constructed exactly in the opposite manner with the point facing downward. Not even the clumsiest Olmec sculptor could have missed this basic feline identification mark—and Olmec sculptors were not clumsy. The drooping mouth and the flat nose together, after one has examined a few species of snakes head-on, are obviously serpentine.

The Olmec maize planters looked at a snake and were fascinated. The over-all appearance of the reptile provided for its association with maize; the people themselves were sustained by the divine powers of maize. Moreover, the men discovered that their own procreative potency was contained in strikingly serpentlike shapes. Then, the mouths of their babies, as their own, resembled the drooping mouths of the snakes. So, for the sake of greater identification with their divine reptiles, they exaggerated the similarities in their sculptures. The peculiar Olmec art style speaks thus of a mysticism by which maize, serpents, men, basalt, and eventually green stones, blended into a harmonious and coherent world picture.

While the task of identifying specific basalt statues with specific serpent species must here be omitted, I am nevertheless convinced that we are dealing with lithic serpent heads and with ancient sculptors who in due time knew themselves to belong among the serpent kind of people. Different colossal heads may go with different species of snakes. But since these heads are also anthropomorphic and were meant to represent divine personages—and/or their priests who rule over serpents, mankind, and everything else—very detailed features of serpent species cannot be expected. We can expect, however, that now and then an artist-priest was more explicit and engraved some more obvious markings. My conviction that this may be so rests in part on the discovery of some such specific identification marks where one would least expect them—in the supposedly very stylized mosaic masks which will be the subject matter of our next chapter.

Fig. 27.—La Venta: Altar 4. *(Drawn after Bernal, 1969)*

From the Izapa sequence in our diagram we can see that in due time the female stone opened her mouth (Fig. 23). In Monument 2 a male stone found room inside. An early version of this idea at La Venta can be recognized in the case of Altar 7. Moreover, at La Venta the female stones eventually became huge altars (Fig. 27). The male figure in the mouth of the female stone emerges increasingly into clearer view until his function is made unmistakably clear—the male Serpent-person literally "presents" his baby. With the passage of time this religion would naturally imply human indebtedness to the deity; so it is quite conceivable that the god eventually demanded sacrificial children in return.

Masculine beings seldom remain continuously in a female environment. A cult which is supported by men's associations, as the Olmec evidence suggests, will sooner or later try to explain the world order with predominantly masculine symbolism. After this fashion, the Olmec Snake men emerged and assumed a posture outside of the female mouth. Their legs

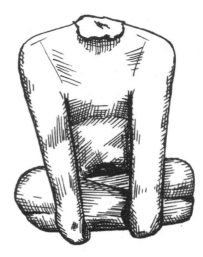

Fig. 28.—La Venta: Monument 73. *(Drawn after CUCARF 5, 1968)*

intertwined after the coiled fashion of snake tails (Figs. 28, 29). This position has every indication of having been a frequent ceremonial posture in Olmec religion, especially during Stage I. The members of the Snake men society sat as independent serpent coils, each forming his own creative and "toothfree" coil—a self-sufficient replica of the male-in-mouth prototype.[2]

The Olmec snake coil position approximates some yoga positions of India. I see presently no reason for postulating a direct diffusion from there, but I cannot help wondering about the extent to which the divine cobra has been imitated by India's yoga masters.[3] A historical inquiry concerning this question will probably have to begin with a search for the reptilian archetypes of Kundalini yoga, with a look at the pre-Aryan yogic "Shiva" figure and a survey of serpent-entwined Shiva representations in later Hinduism.

[2] This Olmec ceremonial posture can be recognized again in a two-foot-tall Mississippian marble effigy, of about A.D. 1400. Etowah Mounds Museum, Cartersville, Georgia.

[3] The frequent sculpturing in Thailand (eleventh–fourteenth centuries, but still in use) of the meditating Buddha sitting on the coils of a large seven-headed cobra, which rises behind the human figure in a similar upright posture, points to this association.

Fig. 29.—La Venta: unnumbered figure. *(Photo from CUCARF 1, 1965)*

Fig. 30.—San Martín Pajapán. A similar sculpture has recently
been found at La Venta. *(Drawn after Bernal, 1969)*

The Olmec squatting or kneeling figures which seem to grasp a bar on the floor in front of them are clearly derivations of the coil posture. The Necaxa "jade tiger" (Fig. 2) stylistically belongs still further down the line from the Saint Martin specimen (Fig. 30). A clue to the meaning of their original posture is given in La Venta Altar 4 (Fig. 27). There a Snake man sits; one hand rests on the body of an all-encircling snake. The man's right leg, on which his other hand rests, is aligned as if it were a continuation of the snake's body. When this Snake person was later disassociated from the serpentine mouth, he and his descendants kept holding on to the body of the encircling snake, but a short block was substituted.

The process of man identifying with and becoming the Serpent deity is indicated in the development of several Olmec iconographic strains. The fact of being in a mouth itself indicates that, futuristically speaking, the eater and the eaten will constitute one kind of essence. At this point of mysticism, in every religion, the embracing deity and the embraced become one. This religious fact is the reason why I see no point in arguing whether Olmec anthropomorphic statues or heads represent gods or men. The answer is that they represent both, because in the ultimate religious consciousness they are one and the same.

Conflict arose, however, when a specific mediator between men and the Serpent insisted on his human individuality. For the sake of prestige and power he gladly identified with the god, but then, instead of living up to the implications of his claim he postponed his own ultimate surrender as close to the natural deadline as possible. Eventually in ancient Mexico he found substitutes who would act out for him his pretended devotion and religious surrender.

The finding of substitute victims in human history degenerates frequently into a tyrannical sacrificial cult. The process is the same in ideological mass killings in modern world wars as it was in the mass sacrifices of Aztec Mexico: this is the road by which mediator-priests become rulers and tyrants. A movement in this direction can be sensed with regard to the Olmec colossal heads. The climax of this development in Stage I can be seen reflected in La Venta Stela 2 (Fig. 23, No. 20).

This stela is the portrait of a hat—a symbol of prestige and power which had grown to the immense proportion of doubling a man's size. I cannot prove my interpretation of this stela, but it seems to me very probable that the person whose likeness is carved on it is responsible for the end of Stage I. From the discussion below it will become evident that among the Snake men of the reform period which followed, a more democratic relationship prevailed. During that time, at least for a while, the chiefs thought of themselves as laborers. Their jade figurines were indistinguishable from those of the remaining members of the brotherhood.

This democratic and humanistic undercurrent is reflected in Olmec sculptures as a process of freeing the hands. Snakes have no hands. Therefore, men who know themselves to be Snake men have to come up with some stylistic adjustments which explain the presence of their hands and arms. It has already been shown how in many Olmec seated figures the legs are intertwined after the fashion of serpent coils. The hands have undergone a more radical adjustment.

Early statues, together with later archaisms such as La Venta Monument 12, do not even bother to show hands; the hooded jade figurine from the south side of La Venta has hands in the form of serpent tails touching at his breast (Fig. 23, No. 16f.). The probably late initiation ceremony which is depicted on a stela from Tres Zapotes shows the same serpentine tails in the place of human hands (Fig. 31). The kneeling figure of a so-called "athlete," San Lorenzo Monument 34, presents a unique solution to the problem of Snake men's arms (Fig. 23, No. 19). I cannot see at all in these shoulder plates, as has been suggested, provisions for attaching movable arms. These are serpent coils—limbs of a Snake man at a position of rest. A comparison on our diagram (Fig. 23) of numbers 14 and 18 will reveal more clearly the struggle for freeing the arms. The figures which are numbered 17 and 18 on the diagram have been "positively" identified by scholars as monkeys. Monkeys may have lived in the trees of La Venta, but these figures, to me, are representations of phallic Snake men. Olmec iconography is very much of one piece.

The famous figure from Santa María Uxpanapa (Fig. 23, No. 22) is generally described as the "Wrestler." I agree with

Fig. 31.—Tres Zapotes: Stela D. (BAE Bulletin 138)

this designation as long as I may interpret the objective of his wrestling by way of a historical allegory. The man "wrestles" to become a humanoid kind of Snake man—to be able to use his hands freely. This emancipation of the hands, which the Stage I autocratic ruler on Stela 2 had already accomplished for himself, is in Stage II to be shared equally by all members of the La Venta Snake society. All this leads straight to the subject matter of the Green Reform.

V

THE GREEN REFORM

1. Serpentine and Jade

Earlier in this study Stage II was identified in the general La Venta sequence. What follows here is an introduction to the new religious horizon which has dawned on the Olmec people during this stage. Two methods of presenting the materials of this most colorful era in Olmec history lie open to me, a timid one and a bold one. Were I to be careful to advance only ideas of which I am absolutely certain, I would have to present the religious symbolism in one chapter and speculate on the chronological sequence in another. But then, an interpretation of religious symbols generally receives its vitality in the context of real life or at least in a minimum framework of historical sequence. For the sake of vitality of presentation I shall take the risk of combining the two aspects.

Chronology has been established better at the San Lorenzo site; religious symbolism is more plentiful in the publications on La Venta. In combining two structurally incomparable sets, a scholar gambles his reputation. But the case for comparison is not as hopeless as it may seem at first. There are indeed some basic similarities between the two great Olmec sites. It has already been shown how the topographical outlines of their central complexes correspond. But this is not all. Both sites have yielded similar basalt monuments, and at both places, as elsewhere, many of these monuments have been purposively damaged. Concerning the Tres Zapotes monuments Stirling has said that all have suffered intentional mutilation (Stirling, 1943, p. 11). Drucker, Heizer and Squier

(1959, pp. 229f.) counted twenty-four "clear-cut cases of mutilation" at La Venta. Since the jade deposits at La Venta came from the late construction phases, the archaeologists suspect invasion. Presumably, anyone who so lavishly buries precious serpentine and jade would not destroy basalt statues.

At this point the religionist evaluates archaeological treasures differently from museum-oriented archaeologists. As a matter of fact, the later depositers of jade and serpentine are excellent candidates for having been the destroyers of the more ancient basalt monuments. The evidence from San Lorenzo speaks against an invasion from the outside. Michael Coe has excavated his destroyed monuments there with great care. He discovered that all these monuments were buried some time around 900 B.C. along ridges and in specially selected fills (Coe, 1968, p. 86). Invaders generally do not bury their ruins; so Coe thinks about an event similar to 1956 when the Hungarians toppled the statue of Stalin in Budapest.[1]

Whatever questions still remain about dating the mutilation of Olmec monuments, Olmec iconoclasm was not like the downing of a single dictator's statue. On only this minor point I cannot agree with Coe. Centuries of artistic creations are rarely linked with single political dictators. Not all statues in Hungary were destroyed in 1956. The Olmec data resemble more closely the destruction of icons which in some places of Europe followed in the wake of the Protestant Reformation. Sacred images of a rejected religion are easily rediscovered as demons and devils by the next one. Why were the damaged statues so carefully buried at San Lorenzo? The answer is perhaps twofold. Since the statues, while they had become demonical, were still those of serpent personages, they belonged naturally underground. And then, just in case they were not as dead as they seemed—as snakes rarely are with the first blow—they had to be put away in an orderly manner.[2] The fact that portions of a so-called "basalt drain"

[1]Two years later Coe (1970, p. 28) admitted the possibility of Nacaste invaders. For our present purpose, the Green Reform implies contacts with more distant peoples when the Olmecs went in search of jades and serpentine. Coe's date of 900 B.C. is a few centuries earlier than I would suspect for the La Venta Green Reform. For the Olmecs the reform may have come in waves.

[2]Some buried monuments at La Venta are associated with a radiocarbon date of 510

have been disposed of with that same care, leads me to suspect that these drains (one has recently been found also at La Venta in Stage I territory) were regarded also as lithic incarnations of the great Serpent. This is what drains look like anyhow.

All this explains at least in part the "How" of Olmec iconoclasm, but not yet the complete "Why." If we assume that this destructiveness and violence were associated directly with a religious reform, what were the motivating ideas of this reform?

Ideas are difficult to lay bare with spades, but the materially expressed symbols of at least some ideas have been found. The first clue to the motivating fascination of the Green Reform comes from the material which was predominantly used—green serpentine rock. In order to obtain this new material the La Ventans had to approximately double the length of their transportation route (Fig. 22). There must have been some reason for their willingness to walk forty or fifty extra miles. The basic idea connected with their new kind of raw material is suggested already by its English name. "Serpentine rock," like its Greek equivalent *lithos ophites*, is named after snakes.

It has been said that the work of comparative linguists compares with walking along the edge of a steep cliff; occasionally one of them plunges headlong into the ravine. What, after all, has the English and the Greek language to do with ancient Olmec ideas? The answer is an honest "not much." But what I am doing here is not linguistics at all; I take from linguistics only a hint as to what ideas have occurred to people who were looking at this particular kind of rock. The Greeks, for instance, went much further than just naming the mineral after snakes; they used its substance against snake poison, and Dioscorides recommended it even for the prevention of snake bites (Faust, 1962, p. 3). English-speaking geologists, not going quite that far, nevertheless named this rock "serpentine."

B.C. (Heizer, Graham, and Napton, 1968, p. 151). Allowing for a moderate margin of error, this could be a realistic date of the iconoclasm at La Venta and thus of the beginning of the Green Reform.

Up to this point we are still not confronted with a basically new idea among the Reform Olmecs of Stage II. In getting serpentine rock they were still dealing with Snake substance; the same can already be said about their earlier use of basalt. But one thing is different now. The new serpentine substance is green.

Because of still insufficient excavation, the historical break between the use of basalt and green substances, such as green schist, jade, and serpentine, is unfortunately not yet very clear. Some serpentine and schist pieces have recently been discovered on the Stirling Acropolis at La Venta, an area which from lack of data I have combined into Stage I. Nevertheless, the general transition from dark to green rocks at both San Lorenzo and La Venta is clearly in evidence around the possible time of the reform. I therefore suggest that the snakelike appearance of these new materials constitutes a link with previous Olmec tradition. Without such a continuity the reform would have to be called "revolution." The emphasis on *green* rocks, however, expresses a new trend and refinement in the Olmec Serpent cult. Green implied a corresponding emphasis on the relationship between rocks and vegetation. The reform, therefore, appears to have been the result of discovering a new manifestation of the great Earth Serpent. The Serpent of the reform movement was green; and the Snake people of La Venta undertook no less a task than to transform their local portion of the Earth Serpent into a green one.

As a by-product, this interpretation suddenly sheds new light on a type of religious fascination which is rather unique all over Middle America (if for the time being one discounts China), namely, the fascination for jade. Unique is this fascination especially when it is contrasted with the fascination for gold of the Spanish conquerors since Cortés. So for example, in the early years before the Spanish presence in Middle America had deteriorated into violent conquest, Montezuma was for a long time treated by Cortés as an honored guest.

Cortés and Montezuma were accustomed to play each day a native game which in many ways resembles chess. . . . It was their further custom at the close of each day's game to present each other with some gift. At the close of one day's game the Aztec monarch presented Cortés with several large discs of gold and silver handsomely worked. Cortés was greatly pleased and so expressed himself. Montezuma smiled and said: The gift of tomorrow shall be such that today's gift will seem in value and preciousness, when compared with it, as no more than a single stone tile of the roadway. . . . The royal treasurer of Montezuma brought in on a golden salver the royal gift, four small carved jade beads. The bitter disappointment of Cortés was so great that he could scarcely conceal it. (Willard, 1926, pp. 146 f.)

Why has jade become so precious in Middle America? The answer to this question is given in Olmec religion. Jades are found in serpentine metamorphic strata. Geological strata, in vertical cuts, appear to have the form of serpents. Thus, if ordinary green layers of serpentine rock represented the Green Serpent's body, jades and better grades of serpentine signified the cores of the serpentine essence—the Green Serpent's bones and teeth.[3] The fascination for bluish jade is also explained by the fact that bodies of water are blue and that all snakes turn bluish before shedding their skins; blue signifies therefore aquatic and serpentine rejuvenation. This interpretation of the Olmec and the later Middle American fascination for jade meshes well with what Coe has already postulated—an expansion or spread of Olmec culture along jade and serpentine trade routes (Coe, 1968, pp. 94, 103). Personally I am not sure whether the "trade" aspect has been of great importance. In the beginning of a fascination, as long as only one group desires an item, the people can usually obtain it free for simply picking it up. I am inclined to suggest that these routes were traveled by people on pilgrimages for jade and serpentine.

Aside from the discovery of the Green Serpent, the La Venta reform movement shows another peculiar development. Having discarded their basaltian and volcanic past, the

---

[3]Some ceremonial stones which have been found in the *sipapu* holes of prehistoric Pueblo kivas have a greenish color. Moreover, the general fascination among Indians of the Southwest for turquoise may also derive from this root.

Olmec iconoclasts abandoned their ceremonial site in front of the volcanic Earth Serpent and dug in at his neck. This indeed makes sense. If an inherited monster from the past happens to be a gigantic serpent, the safest place to be is on his neck. There you are still with him, but he cannot bite you.

From their vantage point on the Serpent's neck, the Green Reformers literally transformed their Earth Serpent into a green one. This took some doing and much effort, which later to some archaeologists looked like a "conspicuous waste of labor and materials." In order to change the nature of the by now frightful volcanic Earth Serpent, the Olmec Snake people had to dig deep. Somewhat after the manner of modern plastic surgeons, they inserted green serpentine into the monster's body—to give him no less than five huge green serpentine mouths or faces. This refinement in materials could not help but imply also a refined planter pietism in the Olmec Serpent religion. The greater emphasis which was put on depth, on getting inside the Serpent's body, represents a physical working out of Green Serpent mysticism—a desire of religious agriculturists to be "in Him." This mode of religious expression stands in direct contrast to the autocratic basalt statues of Stage I which prior to their destruction and burial had been standing around on the "outside."

2. A Mosaic Mask

During the La Venta construction of the Stage II, Period I features, the ceremonial court which lies between the long mounds (A–4 and A–5) appears to have been in the keeping of a ceremonial chief. The burial mound (A–3) of this chief was erected later in the northern portion of his plaza. This man, if he was not the first leader of the La Venta Green Reform, at least was the one who institutionalized it as a cult (or pain) in the Earth Serpent's neck.

In the southern half of this Period I ceremonial court, on the center line of the natural ridge, a cache of 253 green serpentine rocks was buried. Some of these rocks had been crudely shaped in the form of celts. The area over which these

Fig. 32.—La Venta: Mosaic Face 2. (BAE Bulletin 153)

objects were deposited measures 1.5 meters across (Drucker, 1952, p. 75). This green serpentine deposit, it seems to me, has been the first "plastic surgery" in the Great Serpent's body. A more significant deposit of serpentine rocks soon followed.

Immediately north of the first serpentine deposit, approximately at the center of the Period I ceremonial court (at a time when Mound A–3 had not yet been built) another pit was dug, 1.8 meters deep and over 4 meters square. On the leveled bottom of this pit the man in charge outlined a face. With the assistance of his fellow cult members he laid out what later was discovered and called a "mosaic pavement," a pattern of rectangular green serpentine slabs (Fig. 32). After the face had been finished the pit was filled up again, and all those who came past that place between then and the time of its excavation were none the wiser.

What could be the meaning of this buried so-called "pavement mask"? Possibly it could have been conceived as a mask, but certainly it was never intended as pavement. The Stone Age Olmecs really had no need for cobblestone pavements. The reason for the "cobblestone technique" is not hard to come by. Because the La Ventans carried their green serpentine rocks clear across the Isthmus, they probably shaped these rocks right at the quarry so that they would not have to carry unnecessary weight. The pavement idea thus discarded, what kind of mask or face was it meant to be? Drucker called the first "pavement" he found a "tigre mask" (Drucker, 1952, p. 53). The name stuck for all three mosaic faces found to date at La Venta.

There are several difficulties contained in the "tigre mask" interpretation. Obviously, a stylized face is a face, and art critics can argue indefinitely about stylistic intentions. Nevertheless, the jaguar theory has several strikes against it, while the face of a certain serpent matches the mask much better. First of all, jaguars are not green, and for their representations brown sandstone from neighboring regions would have served the purpose much better; at the same time, some snakes are green. Second, jaguars do not wear serpentine patterns; all snakes do. Third, jaguars do not have a cleft forehead, all snakes do. Fourth, jaguars do not have a face where chin and nose run together, their hourglass facial lines are nowhere indicated in this mosaic; many rattlesnake species have what appears as continuous chin and nose plates. Fifth, jaguars do not belong in the ground; snakes are at home in the earth. Sixth, the idea of constructing a portrait in mosaic technique is itself suggested by copying the scale pattern of a rattlesnake body. Still another reason for interpreting this mask as a serpent face will come to light below, when we discuss mosaic masks of the subsequent building phase, Period II.

There are strong indications that the Green Reformer lies buried at the center of Mound A–3. From subsequent developments at La Venta we know that his influence has spread far beyond his burial rites. With the construction of his burial mound, practically half of the Period I plaza was obstructed. His followers, filled with serpentine devotion, moved northward, and, orienting themselves by their master's tomb they planned a new ceremonial court. Their new construction site was much smaller than the previous one; instead, it went deeper. The next leader surpassed this reformer's devotion to the Green Serpent; he and his men penetrated ever deeper into the Serpent's neck. There, deep in the island's central ridge, they deposited many hundreds of tons of imported rock. Green serpentine and jade deposits are the enduring monuments of their serpentine devotion.

3. Underground Serpent Sculptures

For every Confucius there is a Mencius, for every Jesus a Saint Paul, and for every Saint Francis an Ugolino. The Green Reformer also had a successor. Since we do not know his real name, I shall refer simply to his role in the history of the Green Reform—he was the Successor.

This Successor, of course, was not only someone who succeeded a great man, he was great in his own right. His jade figurine, which is probably the one found in the sarcophagus of Tomb B, introduces him as the first leader of Snake men with emancipated hands. He was the great architect of the Period II, possibly also Period III, construction phases. Considering the projects which were completed during his reign, only a leader who was himself endowed with a pair of able and ambitious hands could have inspired the necessary number of workers to participate in his projects. The Successor does not at all appear to have been an autocrat; rather, he looks like one of the people. The spirit of communality soared while he was in charge. The expeditions which he led in search of serpentine rocks and jades must have attracted many aspirants from outside his immediate group. His expeditions must have been exciting pilgrimages, nay, "crusades" for a greener god and homeland.

The 1943 excavation of Pavement Mask No. 1 below the Southeast Platform has been reported by Drucker (1952,

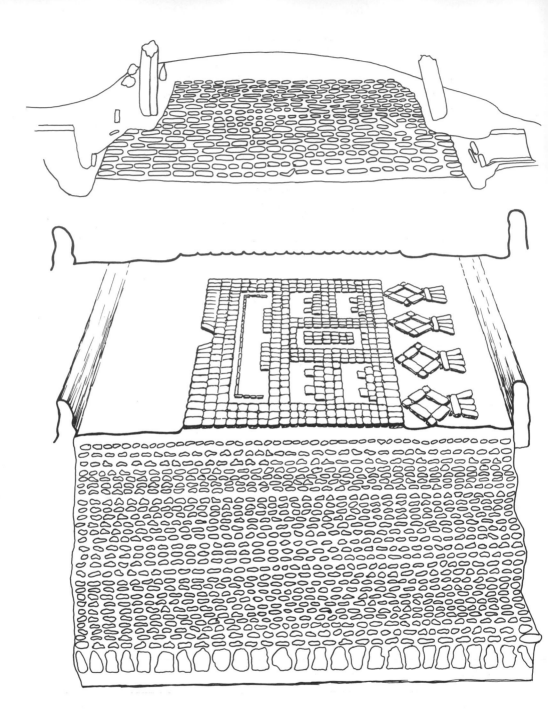

Fig. 33.—La Venta: underground mosaic sculpture (Faces 1 and 3).

pp. 49–59). This find happens to be one of the two mosaic masks which were constructed during the reign of the Successor. The excavators dug as far as the mask, and, after having ascertained that the substratum was also man-made, they let the matter rest there. The serpentine rock creature whose head was left intact will be forever grateful.

Then, in 1959 Drucker, Heizer, and Squier (pp. 78–101) reported the excavation of the parallel mask below the Southwest Platform—the second mosaic mask buried by the Successor. This time the archaeologists did not stop with the face but went as far as the Olmecs had dug to build it. What they found was really amazing. A pit over twenty feet deep had been dug, measuring about forty-one by forty-nine feet at the bottom. Then, from a leveled clay base upward twenty-eight well-arranged levels of green serpentine rocks—about one thousand tons—were embedded in olive and blue clay. The color of the clay matrix, obviously, was chosen to match the green of the serpentine rocks. At the top of this immense square block of "green," the serpentine mosaic face was laid out (Fig. 33). Then the remainder of the pit was filled in with highly contrasting mottled pink clay. On top of this a platform of adobe bricks was built. Basalt columns were eventually added as fences.

With this discovery of depth, the idea of a "mosaic pavement" received a somewhat humorous implication. Why would a one-layer mosaic pavement require a twenty-eight layer base of imported green serpentine rock to support it? The answer to this question is surprisingly simple if we visualize the deposit not as a two-dimensional pavement but as a three-dimensional entity. This is not a pavement, nor is it only a mosaic face. This is fully developed underground mosaic sculpture—perhaps the only such mosaic sculpture on earth.

The attentive observer of Figure 33 will notice that the mosaic face is off center by exactly the height of the diamond ornaments. Quite obviously, these ornaments were not originally planned. Centered well on the green serpentine body, the face was intended to stand alone, as the mosaic face of the previous construction phase, Period I (Fig. 32), had stood. But why were these last minute additions made?

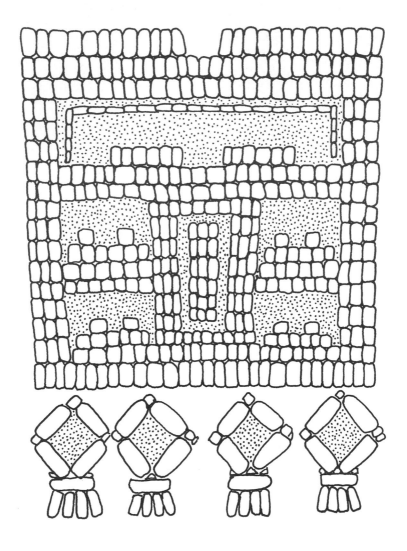

Fig. 34.—La Venta: face of mosaic sculptures. (BAE Bulletin 170)

Fig. 35.—*Crotalus durissus durissus.* Portrait and skin pattern.

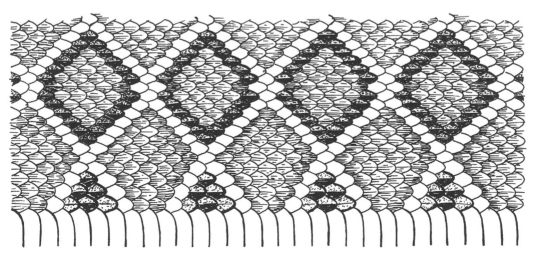

Fig. 36.—*Crotalus durissus durissus*. Lowlands of Middle America.

To answer this question we must first summarize what can be said up to this point about these two mosaic sculptures. From our discussion of the Period I mosaic we know already that the face is that of a serpent. Serpents are associated with the earth; all have a serpentine appearance; all have a cleft on their foreheads; the cheek bone design, heavy eyebrows, the green and serpentine rock, the continuous chin and nose plate, and even the very use of the mosaic technique all point to a greenish rattlesnake. The *Crotalus durissus durissus* from the Mexican lowlands (Figs. 35, 36), as well as the related South American Cascabel, *Crotalus durissus terrificus* (Fig. 37), match the mosaic portrait well. Both snakes have an over-all mosaic pattern of brownish, yellowish, and greenish scales. All these colors link these reptiles with maize. Above, the Aztec Chicomolotzin in Figure 21 lends historical continuity into later times for this interpretation.

Fig. 37.—*Crotalus durissus terrificus*. Central and South America.

Now the answer to our question comes into focus. With a little imagination we can fill the gaps. The ceremonial chief and designer, together with his fellow Snake men, had just about finished the two mosaic sculptures. They were ready to solemnly cover them with earth. Then a visitor, perhaps from a distant place, seems to have come by. With unfeigned astonishment he asked, "What is it?" We must realize that, as far as anyone can tell today, nothing like it had ever been seen in the entire world before that time. The visitor's surprise and wonder is still a familiar reaction among Olmec scholars.

Who could this startled visitor have been? It is anybody's guess. Perhaps it was the chief's relative or competitor from the San Lorenzo ceremonial center; it could even have been the chief's own naïve wife. Personally, I suspect a distant ancestor of Miguel Covarrubias (now that he has been named "Last of the Olmecs" this is possible). In any case, before the

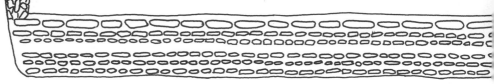

Fig. 38.—La Venta: massive underground serpentine mouth. (BAE Bulletin 170)

visitor went on his way he commented, perhaps jokingly, "Sure looks like a jaguar!"

This did it. No sooner had the disturbing questioner left the sacred grounds than the Successor and his men went to work. For everyone to see they wrote in unmistakable and timeless glyphs a postscript under their two green faces. Their Serpent's name is spelled out with a top-side-bottom view of a rattlesnake! Unfortunately, my camera was unable to copy this all-round view from a life specimen; a drawing is therefore substituted. I advise the more scientific among my readers, when "testing" this explanation, to turn their rattlesnakes with extreme caution. Olmec serpents do not wish to be found out; they would rather bite.

A new discovery can thus be added as an answer to our jaguar question. In addition to not possessing the snake features already enumerated, jaguars do not wear diamonds. The fact that this Olmec "Esperanto" has not been decoded earlier will stand as a lasting reminder of the importance of lions, tigers, and the like, as symbols of religious devotion among the learned men of Western civilization. Then, of course, looking at and publishing these "pavement masks" right side up would certainly have speeded up their identification.

The next spectacular project by Stage II reformers belongs to the territory which was earlier associated with Period III. It constitutes a serpentine deposit in a pit thirteen feet deep and sixty-six by sixty-three feet large at the bottom. On the level bottom of this immense pit six layers of serpentine rocks were embedded, again in green clay mortar.

In this immense underground project the curiosity of well-equipped modern excavators has definitely found its match. What self-respecting archaeologist wants to excavate over 45,000 cubic feet of fill, only to expose a few layers of serpentine rock? Trenches have therefore been dug lengthwise along the center line and from the center eastward past the limits of this massive serpentine deposit. This gives us the extent of the deposit at three points. We cannot therefore be completely sure whether the outline of the total deposit is square or rounded at the corners. Presumably it is square and matches the outlines of the mosaic sculptures (Fig. 38).

Now what can this deposit mean? Have the Olmecs finally succumbed to the "principle of conspicuous waste of labor and materials"? After what we have decoded already, it would seem unwise to jump to such conclusions. The stratigraphic crosscuts which Drucker, Heizer, and Squier have mapped contain sufficient information. Whether the horizontal plane of this deposit is a square or is rounded at its corners is of little consequence; the rim which rises at the edges of the serpentine layers answers our question. These rims are lips, and standing, wondering, or dancing on the filled-in ceremonial plaza above, you are actually standing, wondering, and dancing in the Green Serpent's great and open mouth. Indeed, the followers of the Green Reformer, the Successor and his men who stood by his tomb and contemplated their master's destiny in the mouth of the Serpent, became his devout followers. They would not wait till their time of death to follow him, instead, they would conduct all their ceremonial affairs in the Serpent's mouth while they were still alive.

VI

IN THE SERPENT'S MOUTH

1. Tombs and Burials

In Chapter Three we have seen the mouth of the Earth Serpent traced from the La Venta artificial volcano to the mountain of Tlaloc's paradise in the Teotihuacán mural. Its presence has subsequently been suggested on all Middle American pyramids. Viewing the mouth of the Serpent in its historical development, we see that as the pyramidal coils grew larger, its mouth became more hungry. In the religion of the tenth-century Toltecs, and later among the Aztecs, this hunger of the Serpent was perhaps related to the hunger of a sun deity. With the increasing height of pyramidal heads and coils, the Serpent's mouth could have fused naturally with the sun god of that upward direction. And the two appetites together could devour many more thousands of human victims than could one alone.

It seems rather obvious that the original logic which made human mass sacrifices so reasonable was already inherent in Olmec burial practices. The destiny of man is to be devoured by the Serpent. Middle American human sacrifices, to be sure, were always linked with the agricultural need for reviving vegetation. At the same time, one cannot help but also see an individualistic undercurrent or a heroic quest for meaning in human life. The incarnate culture heroes of Middle America, who in their roles as mediators and priests did the actual sacrificing, had also personal concerns at stake. Being able to sacrifice a human victim lifted them to the level of greater-than-human personages—at least to a level above the sacrificial victims. But this level has not been the upper limit of their aspirations. In killing their victims they beat the mighty Serpent to his prey. Sooner or later he would have devoured these victims anyhow. Implicit in this practice lies the satisfaction that human heroes have actually succeeded in domesticating the Great Serpent. Serpents which are fed by man depend on man. With this knowledge of "limited superiority" over the gods, the Middle American culture hero could actually face up to his own hour of death with honor—to his short passing moments of reversed dependency on the Great Serpent. In this manner, the culture hero could die with a flare of assurance that after his burial he would be an even greater mediator.

Very early manifestations of the great Serpent's mouth may have been the entrances to natural caves. So for example, the Juxtlahuaca Cave, which Michael Coe regards as a typical Olmec site, has at its deepest end a chamber called "Hall of the Serpent" (Coe, 1968, pp. 99f.). This cavity, nearly a mile from the entrance, has been named after a great snake which is painted in bright red on a slab jutting out from the wall of the cave. The snake symbolism of this cave, I believe, can be expanded safely to where the entire cave is seen as the interior of the Great Serpent. The so-called "Hall of the Dead" somewhere along the length of the cave, a place where a dozen or more burials were found, is nothing else but a bulge along the Serpent's digestive tract. The Earth Serpent had been eating.

The Cave Serpent, which at the beginning of Middle American civilization had such great eschatological significance, naturally extended his influence to the origin myths. In the predominantly cyclic concept of time among planter folk the beginning of things will never differ in essence from the destiny of things. Still in the late origin myths of the Aztecs a cave appears to be the interior of the Serpent (Seler, 1961, pp. 3ff.). According to one tradition the first ancestors came from a sevenfold cave in the north. Another version tells that the first Aztecs came from a cave and traveled across the sea. The cave, it should be noted in the illustration, is a serpentlike tunnel (Fig. 39).

The eschatological aspect of the cave is also present in Middle American pyramids of post-Olmecian times. The

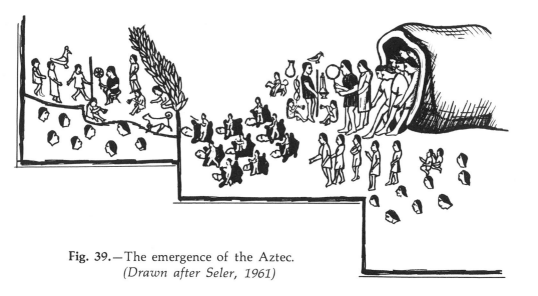

Fig. 39.—The emergence of the Aztec.
(Drawn after Seler, 1961)

eventual significance of pyramids in the sacrificial cult has frequently obscured their original purpose as priestly burial places. J. E. S. Thompson (1954) has told of several pyramid burials in the land of the Mayas. Indicative of Mayan burial ideology is perhaps still the late "High Priest's Grave" at Chichén Itzá which was discovered in 1896 by Edward Thompson (Fig. 40). The chief for whom this "serpent mouth" had been built lies far below in a cave. Subsequently, seven additional burials have been made in the shaft above him. In connection with this evidence, it seems to me, that the universal practice in Middle America of renewing the land and time by covering the pyramids with new mantles has had its origin in the periodic burials of ceremonial chiefs. A new era begins when a new leader takes over, and a new layer on the burial mound was needed in ancient times to cover the latest tomb. This is the manner in which I explain the widening of La Venta's last burial mound (A–2); this is also how I explain for the time being the growth of the great pyramid.

A group of men who were associated with the La Venta Green Reform refused to add another layer to the immense

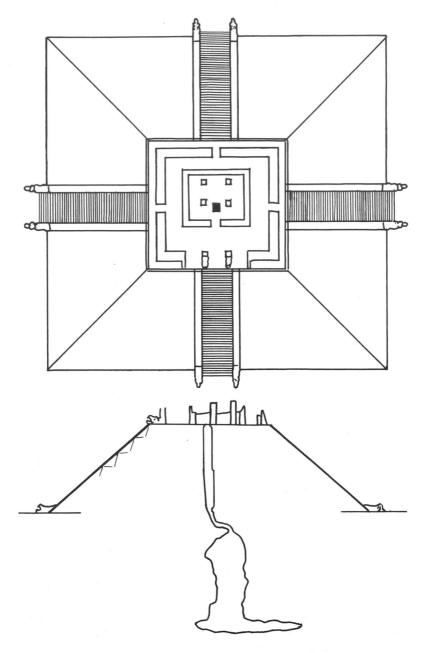

Fig. 40.—Chichén Itzá: tomb of the high priest. *(Drawn after Marquina, 1964)*

pyramid. There are good reasons for suggesting that the population which supported the La Venta center simply grew tired. Each successive burial in the great pyramid required more fill than the preceding one. This stands in an inverse ratio to the general eventual fading of enthusiasm of all religious fascinations. Having to add to the pyramid seemed more and more like slavery. Consequently, the reform movement with its newly discovered Green Serpent drew many followers. For establishing the Green Reform as an institution in history it became important that an alternative to vertical pyramid construction be found. In the name of the Green Serpent, the Green Reformer offered what was needed—horizontal northward expansion and new possibilities for the creative ambitions of men.

The La Venta reformers succeeded in escaping the dreary burden of traditional pyramid construction—the task of enlarging the Serpent's already fearsome head and mouth. They could, however, never escape the Serpent's mouth itself. The Earth Serpent's mouth and its sharp teeth followed the Green Reformer to his new ceremonial site; it remained his most important religious symbol. In the end he died. The Serpent's mouth opened to devour him. But we know from archaeological evidence, that this man's role and influence did not end with his death.

Immediately north of the serpentine mosaic mask, still in the Period I ceremonial court, a mound (A–3) was compiled on a smoothly leveled plane, approximately 2.25 meters high. In the center of that mound a cist of sandstone slabs was constructed. Into this cist the dead master was laid. His corpse was adorned with jade earrings, beads, and other interesting items. The most remarkable item was found in the vicinity of his chest, an 11.5-centimeter-tall jade figurine. The importance of this figurine will become apparent in the next section when we examine the subject of membership in the Snake society. Presently we must examine the symbolism of the Green Reformer's tomb.

Over the chief's corpse was spread a thick layer of bright red cinnabar putty, in the shape of an oval. Around this oval were arranged thirty-seven serpentine and jade celts (Fig. 41).

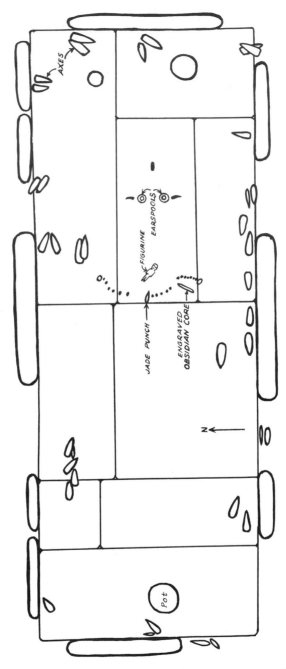

Fig. 41.—La Venta: tomb of the Green Reformer. (BAE Bulletin 153, *1952*)

Three pottery vessels were added outside this oval; one vessel had a crude serpent face modeled on its side.

This burial arrangement is extremely suggestive. A body covered with cinnabar putty suggests envelopment in eternal lifeblood or life essence. Still in late Aztec times chiefs were buried in cinnabar-red cists (i.e., Leonard, 1967, p. 176). But far more important for our understanding of Olmec religion are the thirty-seven jade and serpentine celts which surrounded the cinnabar-red oval and the corpse. These celts, being shaped from the Green Serpent's core substances, represent his teeth. Since later deposits of serpentine and jade celts show signs of having been used as cutting tools, we are confronted here with an ideological association of the Olmec sculptor-priest's tools and the divine Serpent's eternal biting. In full accord with this sculptor/serpent mysticism, the dead chief was laid to rest in the Serpent's mouth surrounded by the Serpent's teeth.

Perhaps a small modification of my interpretation is called for at this point. In the two and one-half millennia which have passed since that burial no bodily remains have survived. Only slight traces of human remains have been found in the most recent La Venta burials of Tomb A. This uncertainty need not bother us, however. Even if the leader's body was deposited elsewhere—which to me seems unlikely—this site would still constitute a true Olmec burial. The man for whom the cist was built was a Snake man. When he left the world of mortal Snake incarnations, he simply crawled back to his home. At least in the form of his most essential aspect, his jade figurine or "Serpent essence," he was returned in his burial to the phallic Serpent matrix from which he had been conceived and born in the first place.

According to investigations by Drucker, Heizer, and Squier (1959, pp. 114f.) the burial mound was eventually covered with a decorated surface. The followers of the buried chief might thus have stood on that surface many times later for regular sequences of rituals. They might have contemplated there the Serpent's mouth into which they themselves were soon to follow. Into the top of this platform, as is the case elsewhere, a number of pits were dug in ancient times. I shall abstain from attributing to them a religious significance. Their chaotic contents could indicate sacrificial pits, but they could equally well be the additions of not-so-religious treasure hunters.

Approximately thirteen meters south of the central burial, toward the edge of the mound but still on the center line, a second burial has been found. Drucker described it as a "child's grave" and added a question mark (Drucker, 1952, pp. 72f.). The plot of cinnabar which marks this burial was much smaller than the man-sized oval of the central burial. No jade figurine was found in direct association with this burial, instead there was a small disc with a scalloped edge. Is this disc the symbol of an uninitiated child? Does it refer to another clan or order of Snake men? Or, is it perhaps the symbol of a human sacrificial victim? I do not know the answer. All I can say is that a similar insignia can be seen on the breast of a San Lorenzo Snake man, Monument 34 (Fig. 23, No. 19).

Subscribing to the sequential scheme which has been introduced already with Figure 6, the reign of the Green Reformer (Period I) came to an end after his burial mound (A-3) had been completed. His successor, to whom the two spectacular mosaic sculptures can be ascribed, could possibly have been buried at the center of the South Central Platform. But since there seems to be no trace of this successor there at the site, it is legitimate to assume that he lived to complete another cycle of construction—a huge underground Serpent mouth, the Northeast and the Northwest platforms, and finally the serpentine basis for his own burial mound (A-2). This second cycle of construction by the Successor has been identified above as Period III.

Thus, it remains questionable whether the end of Period II has actually been marked by a chieftain's burial. This is the reason for estimating the number of successive chiefs in Stage II at "five or six." If there were six, then the Successor's grave was at the center of the South Central Platform and was emptied during the last century or earlier. Perhaps the missing jade figurine is now at the Museum fuer Voelkerkunde at

Vienna.[1] If there were only five burials, Successor I is represented by the figurine which has been found in the sarcophagus on Mound A–2, Tomb B. Be that as it may, in order to simplify this discussion from here on, I shall work with only the presently assured data and skip the South Central Platform in counting burials. Accordingly, I shall refer to the four leaders, whose tombs were found on Mound A–2, as Successors I, II, III, and IV. Their "serpentine identity," with the exception of the poorly documented Successor II, can be traced in Figure 23.

The great significance of the figurine of Successor I (Fig. 23, No. 23) lies in the fact that a whole group of similar free-arm figurines has been found. Taken in this context, Successor I can thus be identified as a former chief of the La Venta Snake society. The relationship of these men to the great Serpent's mouth will be discussed in the next section.

When Successor I had finished the immense underground serpentine mouth during his second construction phase (Period III) (Fig. 38), another pit was dug just north of it, eight feet deep. At the level bottom of this pit, which from south to north measures about forty-five feet, a single layer of green serpentine rock was placed. Precisely above the center of this green serpentine base, on the mound, the sarcophagus of Successor I was buried. This symbolism is explicit. The chief was laid on the same green serpentine matrix to which the toil and the devotion of his life had been given all along.

But this is not all. The sandstone sarcophagus in which he was laid, and in which his jade figurine was found, wore on one end a face (Fig. 23, No. 25). The excavators identified it as that of a jaguar. We now have a better idea of its original meaning. The face is definitely that of a serpent. If the four legs which are indicated at the sides of the sarcophagus are to be given full weight, the face could possibly be that of a lizard. In no case, however, does it score outside the *reptilia* class.

---

[1]Exhibit No. 198. The shortened arms and the position of its hands place this figurine stylistically prior to the one which I have tentatively associated with Successor I but later than the figurine of the Stage II Green Reformer. The specimen was bought by the Vienna museum in 1898 from Dr. Gustav Jurie and is part of the "Widmung Westenholz."

The heavy eyebrows, the cleft in the forehead, the horizontal emphasis in cheeks and chin, and the repeated presence of the split tongue motif, link this face directly to the earlier mosaic masks. Moreover, the decorative style—band ornaments here as elsewhere in Olmec carvings—is far from being devoid of content. For millennia to come, in Middle America, a curved band, twirl, or coil, has been a way of writing "snake." And since Olmec times, the monuments in this part of the world have "snake" written all over them. Thus, according to the revised interpretation of this symbolism, Successor I was laid to rest directly in a replica of the Great Serpent. The general principle which I have applied so frequently in this study— that later representations compensate for the fading of the original vision by being more explicit—holds also in this burial.

The death of Successor I marked the end of the climax of the Green Reform. Successor II was buried immediately north of his predecessor, in the same mound, in Tomb E. His tomb speaks for a crucial period of transition from the Green Reform into an era of religious syncretism. For this reason, the disjointed manner in which this tomb was finally discovered is very unfortunate. Tomb E was the last of those which were found north of the great pyramid. Its northern periphery was disturbed already by the excavation of Tomb A which contained later burials. According to the reports, Tomb E yielded no figurine; but we cannot be certain of this. A broken free-arm figurine has been found somewhere in a radius of two meters south of Tomb A. This radius reaches far into the site of Tomb E, and it is therefore possible that this broken figure represents Successor II. But again we cannot be sure about this.

Two possibilities exist thus with regard to Successor II. If this broken figure had been his, he stood very much in the tradition of his predecessor. If he had no such figurine, he was the first leader of the Counter Reform. That the ceremonial activity at La Venta had been on the decline during the time of his reign can easily be inferred from his burial. To cover the tomb of this leader, eleven basalt columns have been taken from the Periods II and III court enclosure. The people's enthusiasm for importing fresh materials had been lost, and the conservatism of religious devotion, which generally protects sacred sites, had grown so weak that these fence columns could be spared from the ceremonial site for the leader's burial. Moreover, he was buried in a second tomb on his predecessor's mound. Horizontal northward expansion of ceremonial activities, as has been typical of the Green Reform movement, had come to a halt already with the death of Successor I.

The two subsequent burials of Successors III and IV bear witness to an even greater decline in La Venta ceremonialism. In order to build their tomb, thirty-eight more columns were taken from the court enclosure. Religious decline is also apparent in the doubling of their figurines. This subject must be dealt with at greater length below.

The construction of an impressive tomb for himself had for Successor III priority over imitating the Serpent's mouth. In the Green Reformer's tomb we have found an oval arrangement of thirty-seven jade and serpentine celts which signified the Serpent's teeth. With similar thoughts in mind, Successor I was laid in a sarcophagus behind the Serpent's face and mouth; the idea of having been devoured is thus obvious in both cases. After these, the tomb of Successor II contained fifty-nine jade celts which lay scattered, more or less at random, at the bottom of his grave. Finally, from the joint tomb of Successors III and IV no significant number of celts or "serpentine teeth" have been reported. We can therefore infer for the final period of La Venta (Stage II, Period IV) a decline in the importance of serpent-mouth symbolism. This signifies a depreciation in the central symbol of traditional Olmec devotion. This decline in religious conviction among the leaders is otherwise reflected in the disappearance of the society of Snake men from La Venta. This intriguing subject we must examine next. In a manner of turning back the clock, we begin again our discussion with the Green Reformer—at the time when he was still ceremonial chief of the Snake society.

2. The Snake Society

Earlier in this study I derived the two Period II mosaic sculptures (Fig. 33) from the mosaic face (Fig. 32) of the Period I area. Even if my over-all horizontal construction sequence were disregarded, stylistic considerations alone establish this sequence. The same northward direction of stylistic development can also be observed in the case of jade and serpentine figurines from Periods I and II. The figurines which were found on Mound A–3 are clearly prototypes of those which were found farther north.

The Green Reformer's figurine, mentioned in the previous section, was found in his tomb at the center of Mound A–3. The figurines of four of his men have been found near the southern edge of this burial mound. From the archaeological data it is difficult to ascertain whether these four figurines were deposited in association with their owners' burials. Since only a small number of them have been found, burials are a possibility. But even though the precise circumstances of their placement seem to escape us, the figurines themselves tell a lot about the Green Reformer and his men (Fig. 42). Even if we did not know that the figurine on the far left was found in the central cist of Mound A–3, its distinguished pose alone would identify its owner as being superior to the other four. Three of the figurines seem to have belonged to men who were dedicated to manual labor; they are the prototypes of most later La Venta figurines. The squatting figure on the far right represents a devout follower, somewhat more emotionally religious than the rest. The Green Reformer's figurine strikes a noble balance between the workers and the pious one. Ambitious, and yet devout, his image has come down to us from prehistory in the medium of the serpentine reality to which he himself has long since returned. The men who buried him lived to build the spectacular features of the next construction phase. Four of his men, apparently, died before the Period II projects had been finished; they were therefore buried at the edge of their former leader's burial mound. Evidence of others has probably disappeared in the course of two and one-half millennia.[2]

***

[2] Two such figurines of greenish stone are now located at the Museum fuer Voelkerkunde in Munich. They are exhibition numbers 150 and 151 and are said to have come from the Quiché area. No site is named. These figurines are rather crudely made but they resemble remarkably well the style and the posture of the Green Reformer's figurine (Fig. 42). They could easily have been modeled after his figurine by some of his followers. If not, they speak for a wider area touched by the Green Reform.

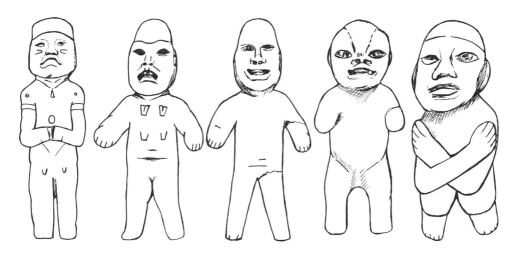

Fig. 42.—La Venta: figurines of the Green Reformer and four of his men.

Successor I, as has been discussed earlier, may have lived through two periods of construction in Stage II. His figurine (Fig. 23, No. 23) has been found in the sandstone sarcophagus at the center of Mound A–2. The figurines of his helpers were deposited at various places in the Period II and Period III construction areas. Some of them have been found. So for instance, the South Central Platform, the place which failed to show traces of the tomb of Successor I, has yielded at its east side, nevertheless, two figurines and an arm of a third (Fig. 43). The first of these, which from an artist's point of view is surely the most intriguing, belonged almost certainly to an aged survivor of the previous construction phase. Among the men of the Green Reformer such a variety of self-expression was still possible. The second figurine is similar to that of Successor I and matches well those many others which were later deposited in the Northeast Platform. Apparently, these two figurines and the fragment of a third signify the burials of men who died during Period III constructions.

Were it only for the burial of figurines which have been mentioned so far, one could not speak of a La Venta Snake society. Fortunately, more information has come to light in

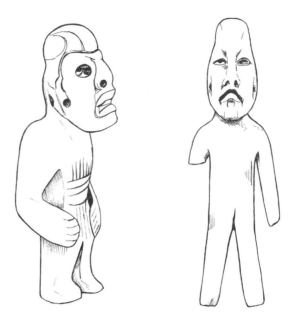

Fig. 43.—La Venta: figurines from eastern half of south central platform.

the famous "Offering No. 4." It is not an exaggeration to say that this find is the Olmec equivalent of a filmstrip in a bomb-proof vault in our time. The category "offering," as applied by the archaeologists, is somewhat unfortunate in that it conjures up the notion of giving a precious "material" gift to a "spiritual" deity. Such a dichotomy certainly did not apply in Olmec religion. Thus, for the archaeological record the term "deposit" would have been more neutral. Nevertheless, all that man does act out religiously is in one sense an "offering." Religion, at its purest, means always man's self-surrender and "offering of self" to the gods. But then, this study of a particular religion can hardly be based on any such general exercises in linguistics. The interpreter of archaeological finds must start with symbolic data that are available, he must be on guard lest he wander too far afield.

"Offering No. 4" contains six jade celts and sixteen jade and serpentine figurines of the free-arm type (Fig. 44). The

Fig. 44.—La Venta: "Offering 4." *(Courtesy Smithsonian Institution)*

figurines match one which has been found in the South Central Platform; they also match the figurine of Successor I in the sandstone sarcophagus. Prototypes of these free-arm figurines can be seen among the men of the Green Reformer (Fig. 42). In style all sixteen figurines of Offering No. 4 are remarkably alike. They, and others which match them, must have been carved within the time span of a single generation. Along this line of reasoning I suspect that the corresponding figurine which was found in the South Central Platform (Fig. 43) was an early one in that time span; the figurine of Successor I, on the other hand, may antedate the leading figurine in Offering No. 4. At this point in my reconstruction I stumble again head on into the muddled data of Tomb E. If the free-arm fragment of a figurine found in the vicinity belongs to that burial, the period of the free-arm figurines in "Offering No. 4" can be extended to include two generations of ceremonial chiefs.

After re-examining their photographs and notes, the excavators surmised that whatever the precise meaning of this group of figurines and celts might be, it represented some important ritual (Drucker, Heizer, and Squier, 1959, p. 156). They could not have been more correct (Fig. 44). Now that we know at least in broad strokes the outline of Olmec ideological history, we can easily decode the meaning of the six celts which define the setting of this suspected ritual. Immediately there comes to mind the celt-surrounded oval of the Green Reformer's tomb (Fig. 41). Thus, the six celts constitute a row of teeth; the ritual takes place at the most sacred place on earth—in the mouth of the serpent. Jade and serpentine together are the essence of the Green Serpent. The figurines belong to that serpent matrix. I therefore consider it sufficiently safe to call their owners "Snake men."

Perhaps it is significant that four of the jade celts show traces of a relief carving (Fig. 45). Apparently they were cut from a single slab of jade. While I have not been able to reconstruct the design from the published diagrams—perhaps matching the celts by similarities in adjacent mineral structures will some day succeed—it seems nevertheless clear that it portrayed a stylized mouth with teeth and a well-attired priest. Thus, in the Snake society of Successor I a definite

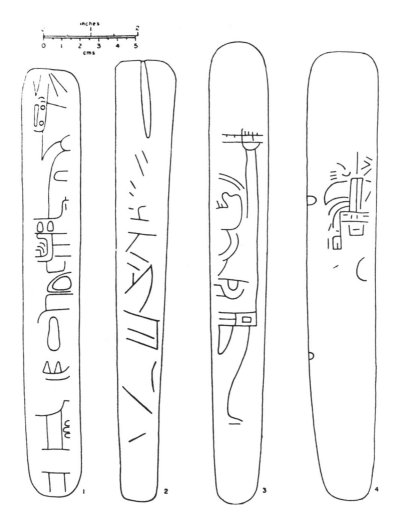

Fig. 45.—La Venta: design on celts from "Offering 4." (BAE Bulletin
170)

trend toward more realistic representations can be observed.
No longer would a two dimensional relief mouth with one
priest suffice; an actual Serpent mouth had to be constructed
in three dimensions for all Snake men to enter.

But then, one row of teeth falls somewhat short of constituting a full mouth. The symbolism is complicated but not
impossible to decipher. The Serpent mouth has, in fact, two
rows of teeth (see Fig. 44). The second row is made up of

figurines 12, 14, 16, 17, 19, 20, 22. The leader of the group, alone, is stationed among the celtlike teeth. Into the open mouth, so defined by jade celts and figurines of cult members, step four newcomers—figurines 8, 9, 10, 11. They are in the process of being devoured by the Serpent. The thoroughness of serpentine mysticism is truly remarkable!

An interesting question has been raised by the careful observation of the excavators. Subsequent to the group's first deposit, a pit had been dug down to the heads of the figurines "to inspect them." Careful examination of the photograph suggests an additional reason why the deposit had been opened. Assuming that the four figurines in the center were added when four men joined the brotherhood, the Serpent's mouth had to be vacated before this could be accomplished. It may well be that figurines 13, 15, 18, 21 stood previously in the center. In order to make room for the newcomers they were relocated behind the humanoid "row of teeth." Rather than disturbing the shape of the original Serpent mouth, a backup row of "humanoid teeth" was begun.

One major question remains to be answered concerning the meaning of these celts and figurines in ritual. Precisely what sort of ritual was celebrated? The interpretation of the obvious aspects seems to be that the ritual in question involved being devoured by the Serpent. Only two types of ceremonies from the repertory of ethnological literature fit this specification—burials and initiations. In discussing the figurine deposits prior to "Offering No. 4" I have leaned toward explaining them as burial deposits. In the case of the latter, however, I am inclined to postulate that it represents a record of initiation and membership in the Snake society. At the same time, a possible link with burial rites cannot be excluded—just as initiation cannot be ruled out for the earlier deposits of figurines.

The question of whether "Offering No. 4" signifies burial or initiation can be answered decisively only in relation to the wider historical context of the last three generations of La Venta Snake men. There is presently no reason to hope for an immediate and complete reconstruction of that portion of Middle American prehistory. I must therefore discuss both possibilities and leave them hanging. Unanswered questions remain in the case of either solution.

Thus, if it be the case that this group of figurines constitutes an assembly of the dead, then the traces of red pigment on them may be related to a burial rite in which corpse and figurine were both covered with red. Subsequent to the burial of the man's body his figurine or Serpent essence was then deposited to join his fellow Snake men in the Serpent's sacred mouth. This suggestion would at the same time explain the perforated figurines of the previous generation of Snake men. The subsequent free-arm figurines could easily have been tied around the body under the arms and so carried, suspended around a man's neck on a necklace. A few missing limbs of figurines in "Offering No. 4" have not been found at the site and could thus have gotten lost during the lifetime of their carriers.

Two problems appear with this solution. First, if this is the afterworld where all Snake men finally met, why did ceremonial leaders get to take their figurines to their respective tombs? The "Offering No. 4" group has a leader still in place, and it seems that stylistically this leader antedates the conventionalized free-arm figurines of Successors III and IV. The latter, being each represented by two different types of figurines, belong obviously to the counter reformation. It is also possible that they belonged to a different kind of men's organization at La Venta. I suspect that the famous basalt stela, Stela 3 (Fig. 23, No. 28), was placed during their reigns; on it are depicted two leaders who got together in some sort of agreement. It may well be that at this event the leader of the Snake men relinquished his number one rank and henceforth chose to be buried in democratic fashion along with his men. This would then partially explain why the number one men of Tomb A each had in his possession two types of figurines. During their reigns they might have functioned only as honorary members of the Snake society.

The second problem which arises with this solution is even more difficult to answer. The setting and the scene of the "Offering No. 4" group suggests an entry of four people at once. Do people die in even numbers of four? The answer would be that this is possible, but also, that ceremonies on behalf of the living more frequently involved groups of novices. It is for this reason that I am somewhat inclined to postulate some initiation rite as the reason for the existence of this congregation of figurines.

Now if one assumes that the ritual which is immortalized by this group of figurines pertains to initiation and membership in the society of Snake men, another set of questions arises. First, what significance can be attributed in an initiation ceremony to the traces of red pigment? An answer to this question is not particularly hard to come by. Initiation into a religious society is always a kind of prefiguration of death. The present ritual signifies death, to which the symbolic setting in the Serpent's mouth testifies, and a subsequent rebirth into a new order of existence. The resurrected men in this case are Snake men.

The second question which arises from postulating an initiation ceremony concerns the motivation for making such a group deposit in the first place. Why, at a given point in time, did it seem necessary to take the personal figurines from the members' chests and deposit them in a communal setting? The most obvious concern responsible for this measure could be the consolidation of membership. During the preceding years of spectacular construction projects, the Green Reform enthusiasm, linked with the experience of going on adventurous jade and serpentine pilgrimages, had involved great numbers of people from over a wide area. Now that the charismatic leader had died and the reform enthusiasm was declining, it has become necessary to stabilize the dwindling remnant of faithful Snake men. At the same time, liturgical reform measures without big construction projects could not prevent the eventual eclipse of Green Reform enthusiasm. Generally speaking, all reforms are narrow and exclusive. Unless later generations of reformers broaden their ideological bases, they will fail to answer all the questions of everyday life. It is possible that the last two leaders of La Venta, Successors III and IV, had become aware of this danger and tried therefore to broaden the Green Reform with elements from Olmec orthodoxy. But syncretistic schemes, concocted by liberal minds, seldom work. There is in religion no substitute for personal conviction and devotion.

A final question related to this initiation scene involves the very survival and presence of this group of figurines. Why were these figurines not picked up for burial when their owners died? The presence of a leader in this group suggests a structural change in La Venta leadership. If the leader of the Snake society—as has been suggested above—was reduced to the number two spot, his continued presence after death among his men is explained.

It is also possible that the entire society of Snake men disappeared from La Venta island with the coming of the counter reform. Their figurines could have been left as "stakes" to their eventual claim on the sacred site. This suggestion, however, has an important factor against it. The burials of Successors III and IV contained two figurines each (Fig. 23, No. 26f.). Successor III is represented by an orthodox seated figure as well as by a standing free-arm figure. It is significant that even his orthodox seated figure belongs, stylistically, still with the free-arm Snake-men type of the reform. Only the last of the La Venta leaders has a seated figurine which differs significantly from the free-arm type; he conformed to the traditions of the Green Reform only with his second and very conventionalized standing figurine. All this speaks of a slow decline of Green Reform enthusiasm, a lessening of serpentine devotion over a period of two or perhaps three generations. In fact, the climax of the reform had been reached at the moment when Successor I was laid into his sandstone sarcophagus.

So it seems that the ceremonial deposit of the "Offering No. 4" group of figurines ceased to be maintained some years after the funeral of Successor I. Under the "enlightened" pressure toward religious syncretism by subsequent leaders, the ceremonial life was stifled and the new ceremonial court neglected. With the decline of reform enthusiasm the number of Snake men dwindled at La Venta, and in the underground realm of the society's serpent essences, action was frozen also. And thanks to the secondary quality of these serpentine essences, their durability, it is still possible two and a half millennia later to capture a glimpse of the Olmec religious world—in the mouth of the Serpent—at a moment when it still struggled for survival.

3. Usurpers of the Sacred Mouth

The central conviction guiding this study is that the earliest stratum of Middle American civilization, the Olmec world, had the volcanic Earth Serpent as its primary deity. I am aware of only five clear instances of Olmec-like feline figures; they were referred to at the beginning of Chapter Two (see note 1) and were assigned there to a late Olmec or a post-Olmecian period. Beyond this, I am presently not in a position to speculate on the exact moment in history when the jaguar first scored in the religious art works of Middle America. Judging from the many references in books on the ancient Maya civilization, it seems possible that a jaguar cult made inroads there soon after the eclipse of the Olmec centers. This is not the place to debate or even to doubt the accuracy of these references. At the same time, the mere presence of the name "jaguar" in archaeological reports is to me no longer convincing. To become convinced I must see the artifacts. As a case in point I will cite the only Maya jaguar deity which is mentioned in J. E. S. Thompson's *The Rise and Fall of Maya Civilization* (1954, pp. 175, 231). Fortunately, a drawing of this deity was given (Fig. 46). Some day, perhaps, after I have had the opportunity to get better acquainted with Maya hieroglyphs, I might agree with this designation as a jaguar god. But for the time being I see "snake" written all over that face.

Whatever the history of Middle American jaguar fascinations contains between the time of the Olmecs and the rise of Aztec Jaguar and Eagle warrior societies, it remains shrouded in a veil of still uncertain and incoherent data. Only a few definite hints seem presently available. Ralph Roys made a distinction between jaguars in early Maya art, where the animal was linked with priesthood, and the Nahua intrusive cult, where the jaguar had become a symbol of the warrior class. For an example of the latter, he pointed to the reliefs and frescoes of the Temple of the Warriors at Chichén Itzá, where various animals are portrayed, symbolizing the Nahua warrior chieftains who ruled over the area. Many of these animals bear human hearts in their claws, suggesting that the warriors whom they represent captured victims for human

Fig. 46.—Palenque: face of the "Jaguar God." *(After J. E. S. Thompson, 1954)*

sacrifice. Here we find the puma, the jaguar, the coyote or fox, and the eagle (Roys, 1967, pp. 198 f.). J. E. S. Thompson, a few years earlier, gave this same interpretation. He pointed out that the Jaguar and Eagle warrior cults were brought to Yucatán from Tula. The Temple of the Warriors had been built at Chichén Itzá about A.D. 1100; it imitates closely an earlier model at Tula (Thompson, 1963, pp. 28 ff.).

The painted walls of a ninth-century Maya building at Bonampak portray warriors wearing several types of head-gear (i.e., Leonard, 1967, pp. 109 ff.). One frequent type is the figure of the jaguar; but there are present also several rep-tilian headgear figures, feathered hats, and other types. All this, together with the above-mentioned variety of predator animals at the Chichén Itzá Temple of the Warriors, points to a multiplicity of warrior societies. It appears that various groups of warriors, fascinated and inspired by different kinds of divine predators, have gradually usurped the earlier type of agricultural men's associations whose primary concern had been the generation of serpentine fertility and life. Rem-nants from an earlier shamanistic hunter culture may have given rise to the formation of these warrior societies. By way of these social changes, resulting from the competition of differently fascinated groups of men and different life-styles, it seems that the act of sacrificing human lives as a technique for revitalizing the agricultural world eventually became an end in itself. The sacrificial cult was modified to the point at which it served more directly the institutionalized interests of the priests and warriors.

The late Olmec *danzante* reliefs of Monte Albán, from as early as perhaps 600 B.C., may point to systematic and even large-scale sacrifices. A number of scholars have already ob-served that the dancing figures resemble very closely the por-traits of sacrificial victims of later times. Their closed eyes indicate that they are dead. The sexual mutilation which is indicated on some of the *danzante* bodies may well represent castration sacrifices (Fig. 47). Some of these victims are de-prived of their serpentine endowments. One of the Chalcat-zingo reliefs, partially reproduced in Figure 23, No. 29, may depict the preliminaries of such a castration sacrifice. The ideological root of castration sacrifices must thus be sought in the Olmec phallus/serpent complex of ideas. What a god gives, he can eventually demand that it be given back.

Whereas in the Olmec tombs there have been found only awls—possible evidences of sacrificial bloodletting—blood flowed freely in later times when eagle and jaguar appetites

Fig. 47.—Monte Albán: Danzantes.

were added to the Serpent cult. As to the gruesome practice of flaying human victims, it seems to me that it, too, could have started innocently enough in the Olmec world of the great Serpent. Shedding an old skin, in popular ancient belief, has been the snake's way of rejuvenating itself. The shape of penes and foreskins, as well as the annual husking of ears of maize may also have affected this cult. At any rate, Xipe Totec is the divine Serpent as manifest while shedding his skin. By the time of the Aztecs, in any case, ceremonial flaying of human victims had sunk to the level of sheer political brutality.

A few good hints about jaguars in the ideological context of late Aztec or Mixtec culture are contained in the Codex Borgia. Eduard Seler has described this document as containing astrological-augural and astronomical matters—the

Fig. 48.—Excerpt from *Codex Borgianus* (18) by Eduard Seler.
(Fondo de Cultura Económica, Mexico, 1963)

latter especially in relation to the motions of the planet Venus
(Seler, 1939, p. 46). He was undoubtedly correct in this state-
ment. At the same time, even the casual observer will see in
the symbolism of the Codex Borgia many illustrations of a
sacrificial cult.

In Chapter Three, I have traced the Olmec Serpent mouth
as far as to the late portrait of a pyramidal mouth in the
Codex Borgia (Fig. 17). It may be of some advantage to examine now more closely the drama of bloody sacrifices which
is portrayed in this magnificent Codex. Tracing this pyramidal

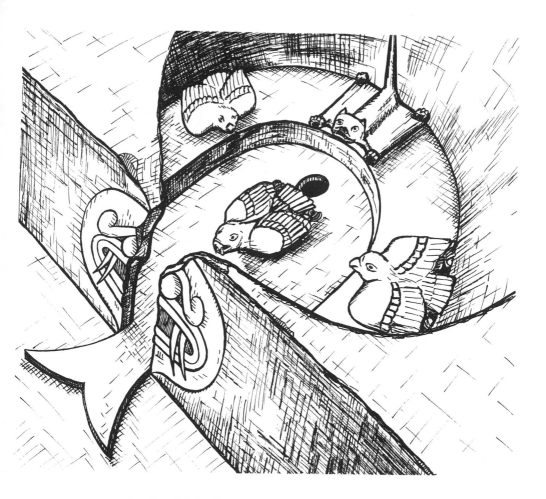

Fig. 49.—Malinalco: temple of jaguar and eagles.

Serpent mouth to an excerpt of Codex Borgia 18, we find that the sacred place has there been occupied by an eagle-owl and a jaguar (Fig. 48). Significantly, the eagle-owl devours the body of a snake. Some usurpers of the Serpent's centrality are thus clearly exposed.

Evidence concerning the identity of two kinds of usurpers is even more obvious in the famous rock-hewn Aztec temple at Malinalco. The entrance opening there is fitted with an all-surrounding serpentine face. The split tongue is indicated at the floor in front of the entrance (Fig. 49). Inside the Serpent's mouth, from the throat, emerges an eagle. Two other

Fig. 50.—Mexico's national emblem since 1821.

eagles and a jaguar are squatting on the bench which extends along the rear half of the interior of the mouth. In this setting it is quite obvious that the Serpent is the primary greater-than-human reality and that eagles and jaguars are derivatives or intruders. Namely, they derive their birth and their authority from the sacred hole of emergence in the Earth Serpent's mouth. Eagles and a jaguar, as depicted here, are the divine tutelaries of priestly Eagle and Jaguar knights. Eventually in Middle America, their claim of having obtained authority from the Serpent was changed to a claim of superiority over him. So for instance, in the myth of the founding of

Fig. 51.—Excerpt from *Codex Borgianus* (19) by Eduard Seler. *(Fondo de Cultura Económica, Mexico, 1963)*

Tehnochtitlán (Caso, 1958, pp. 90 ff.), an eagle holding a snake in his claws became the guiding omen of the Aztecs. This defeat of the ancient Snake by the usurping Eagle has today become fixed in the state symbol of modern Mexico (Fig. 50).[3]

A scene from Codex Borgia 19 is rather puzzling in that the ancient Serpent still devours (Fig. 51). Seler has identified the victim as a rabbit. If one is to put much stock in the length of

[3]For South America, the tendency to displace a still central serpent deity by two large felines may be indicated in the large stone relief from Callejon de Haylas, Peru. Exhibition No. 824, Museum fuer Voelkerkunde, Munich.

Fig. 52.—Excerpt from *Codex Borgianus* (20) by Eduard Seler.
(Fondo de Cultura Económica, Mexico, 1963)

that creature's ears, a rabbit might indeed be intended. But the creature's two large fangs suggest a feline. In the general context of this scene, where blood flows freely everywhere, I am somewhat inclined to accept the carnivorous fangs as being more definitive than the ears. Be that as it may, the creature is being swallowed by the ancient Earth Serpent. Blood gushes from the Serpent's mouth. Blood also spurts from the wound of the human victim and from the wound of the tree. It is obvious who kills the tree and the human victim in this picture—the eagle and the priest's hatchet at the left. Whatever the identity of the creature that is being swallowed, the priest, the eagle, and in this scene also the Earth Serpent of old, function as executioners.

Then, in Codex Borgia 20 the fate of the serpent is reversed (Fig. 52). He is hacked to pieces. In the outside world blood drips from his wounds; his split tongue is exaggerated as if to hint at the purpose of his death. This purpose is explained in

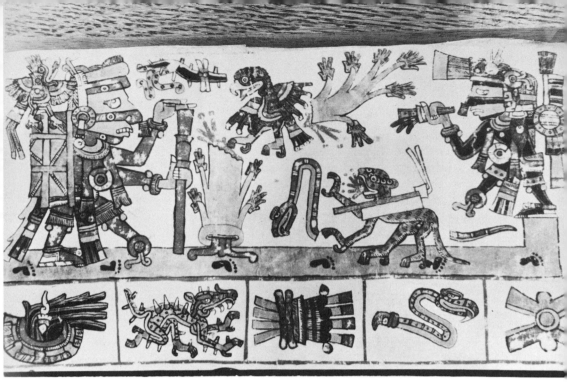

Fig. 53.—Excerpt from *Codex Borgianus* (21) by Eduard Seler.
(Fondo de Cultura Económica, Mexico, 1963)

the underground scene immediately to the left. From the buried serpent's wounds grow "serpent tongues." The plant which at the center has grown upward through the surface is, like every maize plant in the farmer's field, an obvious repetition of serpent tongues. The human victim in the jar is portrayed as though he has died either in place of the serpent or together with it.

From Codex Borgia 21 comes still another scene (Fig. 53). Here again the serpent is sacrificed, in this instance by a feline. As in Codex Borgia 19, the eagle kills the plant. If this over-all scene represents a reversal of the feline/rabbit's fate, we must remain nevertheless unsure. Presently I do not know whether or not the object on the back of the feline animal is a cutting instrument which will eventually sacrifice its bearer.

Far too many symbols in the Codices elude interpretation. Because these artistic representations were originally not intended to serve as books in our sense of the word, but only as mnemonic devices to jog the memories of knowledgeable priests, we will perhaps never decode their full meaning. Nevertheless, the series in the Codex Borgia which I have discussed, which Seler has entitled "The Six Regions of the World," contains an extraordinary number of hacked serpents. Among those who decide about the life and death of the sacred serpents are eagles, eagle-owls, jaguars, and feline animals which may or may not represent jaguars. In the sacred mouths of pyramidal Serpents some of these usurpers have established themselves and have combined the aspirations of hunters and warriors with those of the agricultural enterprise. Sacrificial feasts were amplified not only to achieve greater yields in the field and a greater number of offspring—all this certainly remained a pretext—but also to weaken neighboring tribes, to vanquish enemies, and in the process to enhance one's own might. The element of human self-assertion, which in one form or another is present in all culture types, has thus been amplified beyond its original Olmec religious context to where eventually it has become demonic and self-defeating.

VII

HOW LONG A SERPENT?

1. The Range of the Earth Serpent

Serpent bodies and Serpent heads, constructed as earth ridges and mounds, can be found at various places across the southern half of North America. From a historical perspective it may be said that the early ridges and mounds of the Adena and Hopewell cultures in the Southeast correspond to the later temple platforms and mounds of the Mississippian culture in a parallel manner, just as Olmec ridges and mounds correspond to later Middle American pyramids. This is not the place to solve the geographical origin of any of these cultures. The approximate contemporaneity of the Adena-Hopewell complex in the Southeast with the Olmec presence in southern Mexico can mean formative influences and migrations from either direction.

The circular ridges in Louisiana, South Carolina, and Ohio are reminiscent of the Olmec ridges which enclose ceremonial courts at La Venta and San Lorenzo. That many, if not all, of these ridges and mounds represent Serpent bodies and Serpent mouths stands for me beyond the reaches of doubt. For the benefit of readers who may question this thesis, the builders of the great Ohio Serpent were very explicit (Fig. 54). They located their oval ceremonial court directly in the Serpent's mouth for everyone to see. Better yet, the oval court itself is the upturned orifice of the Earth Serpent's mouth. To illustrate the importance of the Serpent and his mouth, the ancient Ohioans compiled an actual Earth Serpent, four feet high, twenty feet wide, and over twelve hundred feet long.

Fig. 54.—The great serpent mound of Ohio. *(Photograph by Bob Wheaton. Courtesy Cincinnati Historical Society)*

A relationship between the Olmec and the Adena-Hopewell complexes is definitely indicated, if only by the fact that some clay figurines which were found at Poverty Point, Louisiana, feature cleft heads similar to those on Olmec sculptures of about the same time (Stuart, 1972, p. 792). Cleft heads, as we have seen earlier, are distinguishing marks of serpents.

A possible objection to an interpretation of other southeastern ridges as Serpents may be based on the presence of some mounds in North America which are shaped in the form of birds and many other kinds of animals. The existence of such mounds is readily acknowledged, together with the added observation, that most of these variants have been found northward in the direction of Wisconsin. This may in fact mean that the archaic religion of the Earth Serpent weakened steadily as it radiated northward. It gradually blended into the fascinations for nonreptilian animals which prevailed among northern hunters.

While the very earliest Adena Serpent mounds are approximate contemporaries of the Olmec Serpent ridges and heads, the temple mounds of the Mississippian culture (A.D. 700–1700) definitely represent an offspring of subsequent Middle American pyramids. The small number of Hohokam ceremonial mounds, which have been found in the Southwest of the United States, belong in the same category.[1] That a Snake cult with human sacrifices was known during the Mimbres phase of the Mogollon culture seems indicated by a pottery design from there (Fig. 55). Its ancestry in the Olmec relief, Figure 3 above, is rather obvious. Moreover, the practice of killing human beings is once more linked with the cult of the hungry Serpent.

In an earlier chapter I have explained the development of Middle American pyramids as Earth Serpents freeing themselves from their confinement in the earth. Their full length lay eventually coiled above the surface in the form of pyramidal terraces. Together with the emancipation of the Great Serpent from the earth came his affiliation with sky realities— sun, moon, stars—and the amplification of the sacrificial cult by warrior groups which in hunter fashion were fascinated by eagles, jaguars, and other predators. How far the exaggerated Middle American sacrificial cult of emancipated pyramidal Serpents has found its way northward into North America is not very well known. Pyramids have been built in the Southeast as well as in the Southwest. It is also certain that even in historical times human sacrifices were not completely unknown north of Mexico.

Figuratively speaking, the Earth Serpent as a cult symbol may thus have crept northward from Mexico into the south-

---

[1] It is entirely possible that significant burial mounds or pyramids are still awaiting discovery in the Anasazi area.

Fig. 55.—Design on a Mimbres pottery bowl, A.D. 950–1100. Mogollon culture, Southwestern New Mexico. *(Drawn after
a photograph in the Northern Arizona University Slide
Library)*

eastern portion of North America. Then this initial northward
wave of the Earth Serpent religion, which is in evidence in the
Adena-Hopewell cultures, was later followed by a wave of
Middle American emancipated pyramidal Serpents. Another
and perhaps an even more intriguing interpretation is equally
plausible. The southeastern Earth Serpent, as a cult symbol,
may have crawled southward into Mexico in the form of
ridges; he may have returned north in the form of emancipated pyramidal mounds.

If one assumes for the majority of the American Indian
population a gradual infiltration across the Bering Strait over

a time span of at least twenty-five millennia, it seems reasonable to assume also that the people who followed the Mississippi basin in their southward journey were religiously as astute as were those who came earlier and had already entered the tropical regions of the Middle American isthmus. Having thrived for many generations in the snow-capped circumpolar regions, these southbound journey men must have been very startled when somewhere in the middle of North America they saw their first snake. Snakes became more numerous as the people traveled south. The farther south they came, the greater was the variety, the more impressive the sizes, and the more fascinating the colors of these reptiles. In the southern portion of North America and in Middle America the religious people of the New World surrendered to the revelation of the Great Serpent.[2] They were driven into this religious surrender probably, or at least in part, by their increasing dependency on maize—serpentine corn. Eventually the whole world was understood by them as a serpentine reality.

Finally, for the time when the Middle American isthmus had become a bottleneck, a certain amount of northward backflow can be inferred. A wave of cultural repercussions may have reached northward as far as the panhandle of Alaska. In any case, a major wave of this cultural backwash accompanied the northward spread of maize agriculture. It is evident at the same time, that the Serpent and his cult spread northward a little more sluggishly than did maize, the Serpent's plant manifestation. A seed of maize is passed on more easily than is a lifetime of learning about the Great Serpent.

Whether the Adena-Hopewell cultures constitute in the final analysis the local creations of southbound peoples becomes a moot question if one acknowledges continuous intercultural contacts between Middle America and the Southeast. Moreover, whatever culture it was that opened the curtain

---

[2]Beyond this, I am becoming increasingly convinced that Middle American religion must be studied in relation to all the Pacific and circum-Pacific serpent cults: India and China for coastline migrations in the northern hemisphere, the area from India to Australia and over to the Easter Islands for traces of trans-Pacific movements. Some mythic, ritualistic, and artistic aspects of the Australian Kunapipi cult, as reported by the Berndts, match the Olmec data remarkably well.

for the human drama of civilization in the Southeast, it certainly was altered constantly by new drifters from the north, as well as by repercussions from the bottleneck of Middle America. Archaeology will never reconstruct all the ideas and ceremonials of the archaic Serpent cults, it may nevertheless eventually hope to locate more precisely the sacred places at which fascinated people have surrendered to the Great Serpent.

2. The Water Serpent of the Maya

There is no point in wondering here about whether or not the length of the Great Serpent of the Olmecs stretches far beyond the limits of the New World. His mysterious appearance over vast areas in the Americas, at places which are several thousand miles distant from the land of rubber, contains problems enough to warrant a more limited discussion.

In Maya-land the Great Serpent opened his mouth not only at the tops of pyramids, but also as a hungry Water Serpent. The water level in the famous cenote at Chichén Itzá, the Well of Sacrifice, rose and fell with his breathing and blowing. A variety of gifts which in ancient times had been "fed" to this well—copal incense, jade and gold jewelry, pottery artifacts, and many other precious items—have recently been recovered from its bottom. By far the most important gifts to the Water Serpent's mouth at Chichén Itzá were not these precious materials but human lives. In the neighborhood of a hundred skeletons have been brought to the surface by the Edward Thompson expedition (Willard, 1926, p. 114). "Possibly a thousand" more victims have recently been found in a thorough cleaning of the well (Ediger 1971, p. 276). Early in the explorations, seemingly in the upper layers, a number of robust male skeletons were found. This suggests that the Water Serpent was still fed in late times when militaristic campaigns were undertaken to obtain warrior victims. Skeletons of males and females, of children and adults, ranging in all sizes and age groups are among the remains of this unfortunate assembly of sacrificial mediators of divine blessings.

The religious heritage of the ancient Mayas is not yet as

forgotten in Middle America as some people are accustomed to think. Edward Thompson obtained from an old Maya storyteller an extremely interesting account of proceedings at the Chichén Itzá sacred well. The tale is somewhat romanticized but has nevertheless the "true ring" of historical probability about it. An abbreviated version of the story as it is given by Willard (1926, pp. 150–163) goes as follows:

> My grandfather told me this, as his grandfather related it to him, and so on back through many grandfathers. . . . The dwellers of the land were called the children of Kukul Can [the Feathered Serpent]. Afterward the Itzas, who were a mighty people, discovered this city and dwelt about the edge of its Sacred Well for many *katuns* [twenty-year periods]. But before the time of the Itzas, the first dwellers had come to this land in big canoes, from the land of the mountains of fire.[3]
>
> In the city was a highborn maiden, a princess named for a flower, for the very night when she was born, when the goddess Ixchel caressed her beautiful mother and placed in her loving arms a tiny girl child, the *zac nicte* tree growing on the terraced platform of the big house on the hill burst into bloom for the first time and the tiny princess was named for its flowers, Ix-Lol-Nicte—She the Flower of the Sweet Perfume. . . . Sixteen Mays had passed since the girl-child was born to the beautiful mother in the great house on the hill.
>
> . . . So beautiful had the maid become that it seemed the greatest honor in all the land must [surely some day] be hers. She must become the bride of Noh-och Yum Chac, the Rain God, whose place is at the bottom of the Sacred Well. Surely, the god would be pleased with her, for never had he had a bride half so fair. The time was at hand for the wedding of the water-god and a mortal maid. The god who controlled the vase of waters, the dew, and the rain, and at whose will the corn grew lux-

---

[3]Could this oral tradition possibly point to the Tuxtla volcanoes? This reference may be an indirect link between the Olmec volcanic Earth Serpent and the Kukulcán of the Maya.

uriously or withered and died, must be mollified. Each year, if it became evident the Rain God was angry with his people, the most beautiful maiden in the land was chosen to be thrown into the well, to sink quickly to his watery home and become his favorite handmaiden and win his forgiveness for her people.

Ix-Lol-Nicte, being of royal blood, had become the most beautiful maiden in the land. The son of a lesser chief, who was out hunting, chanced into her secluded garden. A secret but innocent love relationship developed between the two. But, above their idyllic love and happiness in the royal garden hung a dark cloud—the probability that the girl would be selected for one of the annual sacrifices to the well. The young man plotted to save his sweetheart. To that effect the high priest's own daughter promised to help the young man. But, caught in the throes of jealousy, this daughter eventually conspired against the lovers. The day of choosing came.

On the great square before the Pyramid of Sacrifice stood the platform of Noh-och Can, the Great Serpent, where would be enacted the ceremony of choosing the betrothed of the Rain God. At the very center of the platform was a massive seat, or throne of carved stone, used in this ceremony since the earliest days of the Sacred City. Over the seat was a gorgeous gold-embroidered canopy with a circular opening in the top, so that the rays of the sun might shine directly upon the person seated there. . . .

At a given point in the solemn rites, the highpriest would call one beautiful maid after another to occupy the sacred seat and the one upon whom the unclouded sun shone longest was the choice of the gods for the betrothal to the Rain God. Thus Ich-Kin, the greatest of the gods, would choose the virgin bride for his brother, the Rain God.

When ten days had passed, the highpriest announced that Ix-Lol-Nicte was in truth the choice of the gods, and soon came the fateful day.

Meanwhile the high priest's daughter, who had promised the lad that she would persuade the underpriests to cast the girl straight into the sacred well, gave them contrary instructions. Befuddled by her words, the slow-witted underpriests failed to fling the victim far enough. She fell on the rocks and her mutilated corpse rolled from there into the green waters.

Her lover, standing at the brink of the well beside the covered bower of the king and poised to dive into the water to aid Ix-Lol-Nicte the moment her lovely head should reappear above the surface, saw her body strike the rocks. Turning like a flash, he rushed to Ix-Ek [the high priest's daughter] and threw her far out into the well as one would throw a small stone. Then he leaped upon the two dazed underpriests and dragged them over the brink so that all three fell like plumets into the water pit.

Horror overcame the high priest and the crowd of spectators. The rain god was angered and with a deluge he swept hundreds of people into his well. Few on that day reached the safety of their homes. The plant which had blossomed first at the moment when Ix-Lol-Nicte was born, and which at every anniversary of her birthday blossomed anew, lay now on the ground.[4]

its gray trunk split and torn and its lovely fragrant blossoms bruised and crushed. But if one had looked closely he might have seen that the heart of the tree had been eaten out by a big, dark worm with stripes of brilliant red, red and vivid as the carmine berries on the breast of Ix-Ek.[5]

3. Echoes from the Hopi Mesas

The religion of the Serpent seems to have reached the plateau of Anasazi-land, on which the realm of the Hopi Indians is

---

[4]The parallelism between plant life and human life is typically agriculturistic.

[5]In the Codex Borgia red stripes identify sacrificial victims. In this story this specific symbolism spells only evil and death.

located, in at least two distinct waves, probably more. But, in consideration of only the aspects of the Serpent cult which have survived till the present day, only two waves of Middle American influence need be discussed in the context of this book. The first wave is still pulsating in the Snake dances of the Snake-clan tradition; the second wave has survived in the Feathered-/or Horned-Serpent ceremonies of the Water and Maize clans.

According to the migration traditions of the Hopi people, from among the seventy-four clans which Fewkes has recorded, ten came from the Utah area up north. A group of twenty-three clans derived from somewhere in southern Arizona (or farther south) and from along the Little Colorado River. Forty-one clans came from the east, mostly from the Río Grande valley (Fewkes, 1897/98, pp. 582 ff.). All of these ancestral Hopi groups planted maize, built houses, lived in pueblos, were influenced by various emanations from the high cultures of Middle America as well as by cultures from the north, and all respected snakes as sacred animals which were somehow causally related to rain and maize. For our present study only the northern and the southern groups of clans require attention. Among the northerners belongs the Snake clan; Water and Maize clans are among those who came from the south. The Snake clan from the north is closely linked with the men's Snake society; it represents thus the early wave of Serpent religion in Hopi-land. Water and Maize clans, with the Feathered Serpent cult, came later from the south.

In the dusk of a Hopi kiva, on a hot summer day, a group of Snake men begin taking out from their jars a number of rattlesnakes. Prayer accompanies their actions. Each man holds several of these snakes in his hands above a bowl of water. There resonates a low noise from the tortoise rattles of these priestly men, and all join in a melodious hum. In accompaniment to this music the reptiles are waved up and down over the water. Gradually the song grows louder until suddenly it bursts forth into a fierce yell. At this moment the heads of the snakes are dipped several times into the liquid, and the animals are then thrown across the room, with great force, upon a patch of sand. In the sand the snakes are rolled and dried (Fewkes, Stephen, and Owens, 1894, pp. 84ff.). In accordance with the rules of kinship and equality among Snake people, as soon as the men arrive at their homes their heads are washed also (Stephen, 1936, p. 762).

On a hot and dry Sunday, in August of 1974, forty-one men from the Snake society and thirty-eight men from the Antelope society, staged a grand performance at Shungopovi, Second Mesa.

On the day of the public finale of the snake ceremony, the whole village is caught up in the excitement. Finally, late in the afternoon the men of the Antelope society—a sister society of the Snake—file into the village square. One after another, each man sprinkles meal and stamps on the board which covers the *sipapu*, the symbolic hole of emergence, to signal the beginning of the ceremony to the inhabitants of the lower world who are about to begin the same ceremony down there. Before the branch hut in which the snakes are being kept the Antelope men walk four rounds. They stand in a semioval before the hut toward the west, south, and east. Behind them, toward the west, a group of women is stationed to later sprinkle corn meal on the dancers and on their snakes.

Dressed in snake-ornamented kilts and with faces blackened, the Snake men enter the arena. On their bodies they wear seashell ornaments, symbols of water. As this group of men coils past the *sipapu* four times, they, too, stamp on the board. At last the Snake men complete the oval which was begun by the Antelopes and stand east, north, and west. Both groups begin to sing together. Several times their song builds up from a quiet low hum to a higher pitched crescendo.

After this song the Antelope men lock arms, and forming a single undulating loop they begin swaying forward and back as they continue singing. Each of these men has the zigzag pattern of a diamondback painted over his breast, shoulders, and back. The Snake men line up in groups of two, a snake carrier and an attendant with an eagle-feather whip together. The pairs approach the hut in dance step. At the hut each carrier picks up a snake and holds it in his mouth; then all three together, carrier, reptile, and attendant, dance on (Fig. 56). The animals are carried between the Snake man's teeth, sev-

Fig. 56.—Hopi snake dance. *(Courtesy Smithsonian Institution)*

eral inches behind the head. With his left arm the dancer supports the animal's body. Fourteen pairs of Snake men keep dancing with their animal kin; thirteen men begin herding the snakes as they are released and as new ones are taken on for each round. Perhaps more than fifty or sixty snakes, mostly rattlers, are used in successive rounds of the dance. The women sprinkle each animal, and each dancing pair of Snake men, over the shoulders of the undulating row of Antelope men, as they pass. The thirteen keepers herd the animals for a while in the sand after they have been danced with. But then, as the number of snakes on the ground increases, in order to avoid total confusion the men begin picking them up by their necks. The snakes are so bundled up into handfuls and carried about. Each bundle of serpents is again sprinkled with corn meal.

When all the snakes have been danced around the plaza, a corn meal circle is sprinkled on the ground and divided into four sections. On it all the serpents are placed, then enveloped in a cloud of corn meal thrown rather generously by the women. Then immediately in a quick scramble, the reptiles are grasped up again. They are again bundled into handfuls and swiftly carried out to the fields.

To conclude the ceremony the remaining Snake men walk again four rounds and stamp the *sipapu* cover in passing— the signal for those below that the ceremony above is being completed. The Antelope men repeat these rounds. They, too, depart as mysteriously silent as they have come. Later, when the carriers return to the village, all Snake men drink a strong emetic brew. They vomit in unison and repeatedly. After all this has duly been accomplished, and with greater detail than can be narrated here, a period of eating and feasting begins. Everyone knows that rain will soon fall.

This Hopi ceremony, nearly two thousand miles and between two and three thousand years distant from the Snake centers of the Olmecs, has constantly been in the back of my mind as I have tried to unravel the archaeological mysteries of Middle America's oldest civilization. In the manner in which phallic/serpentine raindrops fall from clouds in the Chalcatzingo relief, and in the manner in which zigzag "serpent" lightning flashes during thunderstorms, the Hopi Snake men throw their wet serpents onto the dry sand. Rain must fall and maize shall grow in the fields! In addition, the bathing of the snakes and their being carried by the men's teeth is strongly reminiscent of the Middle American rain ceremony which was described in Chapter Four. Then, the use of a snake whip made of eagle feathers points to the familiar dichotomy between eagle and snake in the Codex Borgia and in the Mexican national emblem. Yet, this is still not all that can be said about possible links between Olmec and Hopi religion.

Very fascinating, though in the reports somewhat muddled and not understood, is the subject of the *chamahia*. These, according to Hopi tradition, are remembered both as people and as sacred stone celts. As people, they know the snake ceremonies, they swallow snakes, and they are vaguely associated with Acoma, Laguna, and the distant Land of Red. As spirits they come to the altar in answer to prayers, they

Fig. 57.—Hopi sand altar in the Antelope kiva during the snake ceremony. *(Drawn after Stephen, 1936)*

invoke the clouds. In their concrete form, however, they are ceremonial celts which are placed around a sand painting of the Snake ceremony (Fig. 57). These celts belonged to the Stone people at a time when stones still had speech and life. Now they represent hoe, axe, and weapons of the Great Serpent. In this manner they are also the precious knives of the Chiefs of the Directions—also sacred piercers which had fallen from above (Stephen, 1936, pp. 1208, 707, 625, Plate XVII).

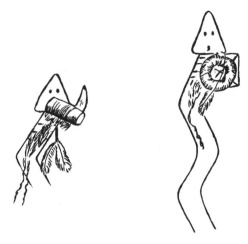

Fig. 58.—Cylinder and annulet, added to the snake figures in the Hopi sand altar. *(Drawn after Stephen, 1936)*

The so-called "St. Andrew's Cross," which can be seen on numerous Olmec statues, appears again in the Hopi sand altar. Apparently it has been derived from the diamond pattern on the backs of rattlesnakes. In the Hopi ritual, specifically, it indicates a female snake. The crescent-shaped counterparts on the two other "lightning snakes," apparently represent hemipenes. These meanings are underscored when, during the ritual, cylinders of willow wood are set on the male images and annulets are placed on the crosses of the females (Fig. 58). That the Hopi St. Andrew's Cross is historically related to the Olmec prototypes seems to me beyond doubt. However, whether in Olmec days this symbol also indicated "female," or whether it referred only to the diamond backs of rattlesnakes in general and to the four directions of the world, I do not know. The Hopi reference in this context to the Chiefs of the Directions, identifies them as the rain-gods of ancient Middle America—thus as extensions and manifestations of the original Olmec Earth Serpent.

All this together belongs to the combined Snake-Antelope cult and specifically to the snake dance. If by comparison one considers the importance which stone axes had among the Olmecs, their function as Serpent's teeth (cf. the Green Reformer's tomb, Fig. 41), and if also one takes into account the later Middle American rites farther north with washing and swallowing—together with the initiatory swallowing of sticks which is practiced in Hopi warrior societies—then the possibility that the Olmec stone and serpent cult could have reverberated this far north, is no longer remote.

The clan myth of the Hopi Snake clan, as it has been told consistently since it was first recorded, is very much adjusted to the Anasazi homeland. The presence of the Colorado River, snakes that exist in a hunter-type mythological prehuman flux, and the place of the first clan marriage, all point in this myth to a local synthesis. We may thus have, preserved in this clan myth, a northerly tributary to the earliest wave of Serpent religion in Hopi-land. (Moreover, this myth may some day help unravel the Anasazi riddle.) The stream which has fed this tributary from the south could have provided such ritualistic aspects as stone celts, snake washing, and vomiting. Whether this early wave of Snake religion in Anasazi-land included a familiarity with human sacrifices, has not been determined. I am inclined to ascribe the Mimbres evidence, in Figure 55, to a later wave of influence from farther south.

The Hopi Snake clan traces its origins to Tacoanavi, a place up north in the vicinity of what is now known as Navajo Mountain. From there the mythical beginnings of the Snake religion are traced all the way down the mighty Colorado River to the ocean. Somewhat later, perhaps because of the adventuresome journey of the Snake hero and the proximity of the Grand Canyon, this clan myth has entered the mythologies of other peoples in the area. A modified version explains the origin of the Navajo Feather Chant, a healing ceremonial. The two Hopi versions which I have at my disposal (Voth, 1905, and Kewanwytewa, 1961) compare with each other very closely.

A lad, curious about where all the water in the Colorado River flows, carved for himself a hollow log. In this log he floated down the river, all the way through the Grand Canyon and on to the ocean. At the farthest point of his journey Spider Woman helped him on several occasions; he was a guest at her kiva.

The point of the story is that the hero eventually found his way to the House of Snakes. From the divine Snake people there he learned all the details about the Snake cult. Then, as a duly initiated Snake person he returned to his people, bringing with him a Snake maiden for his wife. The woman bore him many children; all turned out to be snakes. They bit the children of the village so that they swelled up and died. On account of this the founder of the Hopi Snake clan and cult carried all his snake children back to the homeland of his wife. Together with them the ancestral pair left the village and settled at Walpi. There the woman ceased bearing snakes and instead gave life to human children, namely, to the next generation of ancestors of the Hopi Snake clan. Today the Hopi Snake people, when they have their snake ceremonies, gather up a few of their first brothers and sisters to dance with them. The words of Jimmie Kewanwytewa (1961, p. 10) explain well their present motivation for dancing with snakes:

> . . . other villages have been taking up some of this religion, because they do the Hopis a lot of good. When they dance the snake dance it usually rains very hard to keep the plants growing faster. So that is how they still keep on this snake ceremony each year.

What I have explained already in general terms in Chapter One, and what I have repeated afterward specifically in relation to the Olmecs, applies also in the case of the Hopi Snake cult. "Cult" means never a complete religious surrender or complete harmony; instead, it embodies also the human aggressive response to so-conceived greater-than-human reality configurations. The intrinsic nature of this aggressive response is modified only to the extent that the greater-than-human realities surrender on their own—either through divine self-sacrifice, through grace, or by way of their revealed beneficial nature or neutrality—to the needs and ambitions of men. In this tug of war both gods and men adapt and change their faces.

Contrary to what some neo-Indian spokesmen are saying today, the snake dancers are not in complete harmony with nature. Their manipulation of the snakes signifies a kind of scientific control over so-conceived slightly less-than-human

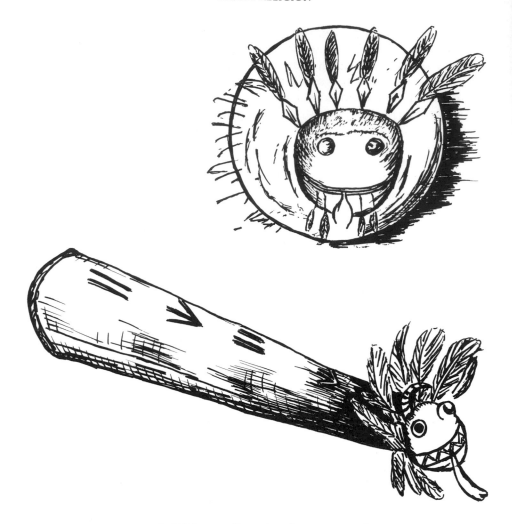

Fig. 59.—Hopi Palülükona effigies used in winter solstice ceremony.
(Drawn after Stephen, 1936)

realities, over the lesser manifestations of the great Serpent on
whom they depend so ultimately. At the same time, I readily
grant that these Hopi Snake men are a good deal closer to
being in harmony with their snake kinfolk than are the pale-
face snake handlers in Appalachia who confront serpents as

manifestations of the devil. The latter seem to handle venomous snakes only to prove that the power of the Biblical serpent bruiser of Genesis 3:15 is under their control.

With the second wave of Middle American influence into Hopi-land came a Maya-type Water Serpent. He is a single as well as a multiple deity. As such he surfaces at many springs and pools in the land of the Pueblo Indians—everywhere except among the Tiwa. In Zuñi he is Kolowisi, Keres people know him as Tsitshrue or Gatoya, to the Tewa he is Avanyo, in Jémez he is Wanakyudy'a, and the Hopi call him Palülükona. At the Water Serpent's feast, during the winter solstice, some of these peoples march in processions to their springs and make offerings of prayer feathers to him. The Zuñi have a tradition that women should never immerse themselves in springs or pools, lest the Water Serpent should impregnate them. During the Serpent's ceremony in the kiva, the symbolic *sipapu*, or hole of emergence, is unplucked and, represented in effigy (Fig. 59), the deity vomits water and seed maize (Parsons, 1939, pp. 184f., 202, 394, 525 and Stephen, 1936, p. 343). For our present purpose it is sufficient if the discussion remains limited to the Water Serpent traditions of the Hopi.

Among the clans from the south, the Water clan ranks first. Closely related to the Water clan and derived from it is the Maize clan. We are very fortunate that several versions of the Water and Maize clan myths have been recorded. For the purpose of rediscovering the Middle American Water Serpent in what are perhaps his northernmost abodes, I shall briefly summarize a few of these myths.

The first version is the clan origin myth of the Water people. It was told to A. M. Stephen by Anawita, a Water clan chief. In order to enable easier comparison later in our discussion, I will divide this myth into two parts.

Part I

We are the Patkinyumu, and we dwelt in the Palatkwabi [Red Land] where the kwani [agave] grows high and plentiful; perhaps it was in the region the Americans call Gila valley, but of that I am not certain. It was far south of here, and a large river flowed past our village, which was large, and the houses were high, and a strange thing happened there.

Our people were not living peaceably at that time; we were quarreling among ourselves, over huts and other things I have heard, but who can tell what caused their quarrels? There was a famous hunter of our people, and he cut off the tips from the antlers of the deer which he killed and he always carried them. He lay down in a hollow in the court of the village, as if he had died, but our people doubted this; they thought he was only shamming death, yet they covered him up with earth. Next day his extended hand protruded, the four fingers erect, and the first day after that one finger disappeared; each day a finger disappeared, until on the fourth day his hand was no longer visible.

Part II

The old people thought that he dug down to the underworld with the horn tips. On the fifth day water spouted up from the hole where his hand had been and it spread over everywhere. On the sixth day Palülükona protruded from this hole and lifted his head high above the water and looked around in every direction. All of the lower land was covered and many were drowned, but most of our people had fled to some knolls not far from the village and which were not yet submerged. When the old men saw Palülükona they asked him what he wanted, because they knew he had caused this flood; and Palülükona said, "I want you to give me a youth and a maiden."

The elders consulted, and then selected the handsomest youth and fairest maid and arrayed them in their finest apparel. . . . These children wept and besought their parents not to send them to Palülükona, but an old chief said, "You must go; do not be afraid; I will guide you." And he led them toward the village court and stood at the edge of the water, but sent the children wading in toward Palülükona, and when they reached the center of the court where Palülükona was the deity the children disappeared. The water then rushed down after them, through a great cavity, and the earth quaked and many houses tumbled down, and from this cavity a great mound of dark rock protruded. This rock mound was glossy and of all colors; it was beautiful, and, as I have been told, it still remains there. (Mindeleff, 1891/92, p. 188.)

Somewhat in contrast to the above myth, the origin myth of the Maize clan tells us more in Part I and is more scanty in Part II. A different type of Middle American sacrifice—not unlike one discovered on the island of Ceram by Jensen—is here crafted into the basic Water-clan myth (cf. Jensen, 1948). The Old Oraibi variant of the Maize-clan story goes like this:

Part I

After our people had emerged from the underworld during a period of migrations, they divided into language groups and clans. Their divine chief, Massau, was afraid that all people would remain together in one lump, so he asked mockingbird to interfere. This bird knows all languages and gave different languages to different groups of people. Immediately after the emergence the Maize clan was still part of the Water clan, but soon its people split off and migrated south.

After this the Maize clan people lived in the Red City of the south. Other Hopi clans lived there too. One night all people put on a dance. They kept on dancing and forgot their duties. On four successive nights the nephew of the chief appeared in the town plaza, masked like a ghost. On the fourth night he was caught and was buried in a hole in the center of the plaza. On four nights thereafter the dead man stuck up his hand through the hole and gave a finger countdown: four, three, two, one . . . .

Part II

Then the deluge came from below; it drove the people from their town. At that time some of the old people were transformed into turkeys. They remained confusedly behind. A brother, with his twin sister, who remained behind also, came to the place where the man had been buried. They were selected by the chief to deliver an offering of prayer feathers. From the grave emerged the

Feathered Serpent and told the twins not to be afraid but to go and release the turkeys. At that occasion Deer offered his meat for the twins to eat and to survive on. Another divine personage gave them various seeds with the necessary instructions about how to plant. Then that same divine personage gave the children a "whirling basket" on which they flew to their people who had fled far away. Having rejoined them the two taught the people what they had learned. This took place en route to the present homeland of the Hopi, somewhere south of Winslow, along the Little Colorado River. From Homolovi, near Winslow, they moved to Walpi and asked four times to be admitted. Four times this was denied. So they moved on to old Shipolovi, at the foot of the mesa on which lies present-day Shipolovi.

It is interesting to note that in the myth of the Water clan the sacrifice to the Water Serpent in Part II is balanced in Part I with the story about a deer hunter. The reverse is true in the Maize clan myth, where the story drifts from a distinct sacrifice in Part I into the general rambling of a hunter-type origin myth in Part II. The portions in each clan myth which narrate a human sacrifice, I take it, constitute their southern-most cores. The hunter elements in both instances appear to have come into the Hopi tradition from a northerly source.

The occurrence of a flood in each of these clan myths represents a significant link with the Maya Water Serpent and the Middle American cenote cult in general. Among the Indians of the Southwest this mythical theme has produced a meaningful echo in what has meanwhile become the myth *par excellence* of this area. The emergence of the first people from stratified cavities in the underworld is now generally understood as having been an escape from the rising waters. The waters would only retreat when a child—usually Water's own child—was thrown into the hole.

It seems thus that the various Hopi clan myths are somewhat older than the by now universal myth of emergence. To be sure, the emergence myth has equally ancient antecedents in Middle America. Emergence in the Southwest is still basically a coming forth from the Serpent's mouth—albeit by now from a toothless mouth or a plain hole. Nevertheless, as the myth of emergence is now generally told, with its four underworlds (Aztec epochs or "suns" cast into categories of space), with a toothless hole and rising waters, it represents in the Hopi context a mythological synthesis that would unify and undergird the societal synthesis of various Hopi clans and religious traditions.

The moral lesson of the clan myths is peripheral to their ontological import; it varies from one informant to another. The version just given hints at a cultic dance and sacrifice which later came into disfavor among the people. In the next version, which will follow below, the flood is being rationalized as punishment for sexual chaos. This idea may stem in part from a Saturnalian type of licence or suspension of rules which is known to have accompanied agriculturistic renewal feasts the world over. It is also significant that the setting of this next version is transferred into a Hopi-like kiva. It appears that in some way the content of this myth was re-enacted in the kiva, probably in accordance with the ceremonial calendar. In this myth, which is obviously a later version, human sacrifices have been reduced to a burial of four kachina masks.[6] Later in the same story the Water Serpent himself becomes the sacrificial victim.

A very angry chief, whose wife had been raped by men of the town, plotted revenge. He gave his nephew four different kinds of kachina masks to wear. Repeatedly, at midnight, the masked man haunted the people of the town and killed whomever he could. A poor boy of the town secretly improved his running skills, and one day, after he had succeeded in catching the masked man, he came dragging him into a kiva. One by one the kachina masks were removed from the captive's face.

One old man assisted the chief. He said: "Dig for me a hole in the middle of this house. Put the masks in it and cover them over; on the top, place a cover. Then watch and see what will happen." The old man told them to dig

---

[6]Elsewhere in Hopi ceremonialism substitutional prayer sticks, some of them still with faces indicated, are placed for the gods.

a *tivo'nyapavi*, a small emergence shrine which no one
will touch. In the morning, all climbed up to the house-
top in order to watch. Four fingers were seen coming out
of the ground at the *tivo'nyapavi*. Next day one went
down and only three were left. On the following day . . .
two were left. Next day . . . one was left. But one day now
remained before the event would take place. All went
where they could observe it. . . . A noise was heard. . . .
It was the old man. He was the dragon [Water Serpent],
having put on the dragon's mask. He came out . . . . The
house trembled. There was an earthquake. About break-
fast time, the earth was shaking and moving about. A
great many people ran away. The earth turned upside
down, and all the people went down beneath it. Then
the rest of the people moved away. Soon the old man
was standing up high in the middle of the house-top.

A boy and a girl were left behind by the fleeing people.
Their grandfather, the Water Serpent, approached them and
spoke:

"Your father and mother are living. Look through the
whole house and you will find something to eat. . . . You
will find a knife somewhere, bring it to me! . . . Leave me
alone here! . . . Follow your mother whom you will find
somewhere. Tell her what I tell you. Take off some of my
flesh here!" he said, pointing to his hip. The boy was not
willing to do so, thinking that it would be painful. "Do
not think it will hurt me. It will not hurt. Take along this
flesh and when you reach your father tell him: 'Some-
times there will be no rain, and the ground will become
dry. Take a small piece of my flesh, grind it up, place it
on the prayer stick and send it to me . . . .'" The boy cut
off a piece of flesh from around the dragon's hip . . . .
They went south, then northeast, then southwest. The
people were now living at Shumopovi. (Wallis, 1936, pp.
17 ff.)

That the Middle American memory of human sacrifices
was overcome by the Hopi people only gradually is supported
by two examples from my personal research notes. The present general decline of Old Oraibi, as it has been explained by

a kiva chief, is the result of the last full chief of Old Oraibi, Lololoma, refusing to have himself sacrificed in a time of great need. This obstinate chief was only one generation removed from people who are still alive. In another instance, it has been whispered that in ancient times the Soyal ceremony, especially one during initiation years (every fourth year), could include a human sacrifice. According to this rumor, a maiden from the Parrot clan was formerly taken into the kiva, was placed on seeds to hatch them, and after certain other ritualistic procedures was finally sacrificed. More recently such practices as washing her hair and giving her a new name have been substituted.

The conclusion should not be drawn that the Hopi people were uniquely involved in the practice of human sacrifice. There is probably no culture or civilization anywhere in the world where at some point in history the "supreme sacrifice" has not been valued. Rather, from all this it can be seen that the humanistic genius of the Hopi people, whose ancestors may well have fled north from the hungry mouths of Middle American Serpents, has won many victories. It is certainly true that one whose livelihood depends on growing maize— or serpent corn— can emancipate himself only with great difficulty from the demands of the great Earth Serpent.[7] Even such part-time maize planters as the Western Apaches need "snake medicine" to raise good crops (Opler, 1972). Historically speaking, it seems to me that the victims of the Serpent themselves— sacrificial victims devoured in former times, but also the recent dead— have banded together in the Hopi world and have wrested from the Serpent his exclusive control over the powers of growth. As *kachina* spirits, many of whom belong to regions above the realm of vegetation, these former victims have widened the Hopi cultural horizon and have liberated the people from their slavery to the hungry Earth Serpent. As saviors they have literally risen from the Serpent's mouth, from the crater of the San Francisco Peaks and from other *sipapus*, to redeem Hopi culture.

---

[7]For additional northward reverberations of the Middle American sacrificial Serpent cult, see Chapter III on "Tlaloc's Paradise" with reference to the San Juan Tewa and their sacred mountains.

In Mexico, as well as in the land of the Hopi, the feathers which have gradually become associated with the Water Serpent illustrate this same humanistic gospel of upward liberation. A world which is understood through the symbolism of serpents as well as of birds implies a wider horizon and a greater living space than does a world of down-to-earth serpents alone. Thus, Topiltzin, a Toltec reform king who assumed the name Quetzalcoatl, "Feathered Serpent," is remembered for his opposition to human sacrifices.

It must at the same time be recognized that an excessive emphasis on bird symbolism alone—especially if the birds involved were eagles or other birds of prey—does not seem to have improved significantly the fortunes of the common people. As the Codex Borgia illustrates, and as the historical roles of Aztec Eagle knights reveal, the greater-than-human Eagle could be as bloodthirsty as the hungry Earth Serpent. The fact that, over against the Aztec horizon of snake-eating birds, eagles were used in Hopi-land primarily as sacrificial animals—while at the same time serpents were revered—signifies another reversal and triumph of the humanistic ideal. Another less-than-anthropomorphic *mysterium tremendum*, which had become oppressive, was defeated.

VIII

A MYTHIC POSTSCRIPT:
Western Scholar in Olmec Paradise

Success in understanding foreign world views depends on a personal perspective broad enough to embrace sincerely many world views. It also depends on the student's willingness to stand on a personal level in other people's shoes. To this end I know of no better discipline than that of rational and emotional participation in the fascinations of other people. The first of these has been accomplished to some degree, I trust, in the preceding pages. But emotional sharing cannot take place without a certain attitude of playfulness.

The primary subject of Olmec fascinations was an animal. Until now this animal was believed to have been a jaguar. In this book I have argued that, in fact, it was a serpent. For only a few final pages I shall now try to leave the seriousness of scholarly debate and follow with my readers the lure of the Muses. I invite my readers to participate with me in ancient jaguar-type and serpent-type fascinations. The story of these fascinations has its origin deep at the very root tips of Western civilization. It therefore needs to be told in a broader mythological context, engulfed in the midst of which scholarship has been wrestling with itself all along. The Western scholar will never succeed in understanding foreign religions until he has learned to face up honestly to his own rich mythico-religious heritage.

Please note that what I am about to tell is not the Olmec story as it might formerly have been told, nor is it the Western story in its orthodox form; rather, it is the revised story of how these two stories have met.

In the beginning—where things usually start—God created human kind. The first human beings lived in paradise until, desirous of culture and civilization, they ate from the forbidden tree of knowledge. In this manner they gained the knowledge of how to distinguish good from evil, but they lost their paradisiac innocence. This required some adjustment on the part of the people. Knowing now the art of analysis, and discovering too many opposites and distinctions about each other, they no longer could trust each other. On their fellow animals they heaped even greater distrust. Here the story gets to the point.

There was a serpent, and there was a jaguar. One of these two was sure to get blamed for the origin of Western civilization, man's estrangement from God. The jaguar saw what was coming up and before he could get accused he fled to Middle America. The serpent was a little slower and, let's face it, a little too archaic; he really caught the blame. The patriarchs of Western civilization heard God speak of enmity between men and serpents. A son of men shall bruise the serpent's head, and the serpent will bite the hero's heel (Gen. 3:15). Ever since the time of the patriarchs the heirs of this divine promise have blamed the serpent for all their ills. They refused to look a snake straight in the face. After a while they even forgot what one looked like.

The jaguar, on the other hand, remained in vivid memory among the peoples of Western civilization. Since he was gone, they bestowed all their affections on the jaguar's larger brother, the lion. People were so fascinated by the lion that they elected him "king of animals." More and more Western men placed their hopes in lion figures—in the Lion of Judah, in lion-hearted knights, in lion-crested cities and taverns, and finally in scholars who were fascinated by lions.

Around the time when these lion-minded scholars began to bud from Europe's monasteries, lion-hearted militiamen discovered and conquered Middle America. They found the Aztec warrior societies at the height of their power—Jaguar warriors and Eagle warriors together. Both animals, the large feline and the bird of prey, were familiar crests of European conquerors.

The remainder of my story is well known from the history of Middle American studies. Who was it that fascinated the lion-hearted and the lion-minded men of Europe in this otherwise unfamiliar land? Of course, the jaguar!

Had the scholars of European descent remained what they once were, scholars in monasteries fascinated by the lamb, they would have remembered some of their more ancient wisdom, namely, that the serpent is more subtle than any animal in the field (Gen. 3:1). Western scholars had grown oblivious to this truth and so fell to the serpent's trick.

It happened in this manner. Soon after the arrival of the jaguar in Middle America, the scorned serpent also found his way there. In the course of several millennia he carefully planned a laugh on his despisers. In the land of rubber trees he found a group of simple maize planters whom word of his defamation had not yet reached. These people were fascinated by the serpent and soon discovered that people, maize plants, snakes, stones, mountains, and ridges belonged all to a single green world. On their sculptured stones, therefore, their own faces blended right in with serpent faces.

The serpent's plot succeeded. Recent Western scholars, knowing that great results come from great causes—measured by Western standards, of course—credited the jaguar, brother of the lion, with having originated the great civilization of Middle America. All the while—for several decades now—in a game of fun the mischievous Olmec serpent was playing hide-and-seek with lion-minded scholars. Until . . . , yes, until a trail was found leading back to the common paradise of both Western and Olmec civilization. There, in that paradise, for the time being the stigma which the fall of Western man has attached to serpent existence was forgotten; we now look this creature straight in the face.

This is the story of how in later time the Olmec serpent was finally discovered. To reach this common paradise where a Western man could face a serpent head-on he had to climb a steep cliff. Ivory towers which stood along the road to this paradise reached high enough, indeed, but they could not bridge the gap. Someone had to climb this cliff. The books of fellow scholars, archaeologists and herpetologists who searched along the same trail, were sufficient in number to be stacked into a makeshift stairway. Then, as a dwarf, standing on the shoulders of scholarly giants, this author could see and reach a little farther.

And in the paradise, where a Western man and the Olmec serpent stood facing each other finally again head-on, God the Creator smiled. He has all along enjoyed the comedy with the performance of which his two-legged, four-legged, and legless animals have kept him entertained through several turbulent millennia. This comedy, I am sure, is what made eternity for him more interesting. And his voice resounding with glorious amusement, God said: "Had Western man listened long ago to my servant Moses when he lifted up the serpent in the wilderness (Num. 21:9), had they learned to look in the face of a serpent then, they would surely have recognized him sooner in Olmec-land."

In the distance of this paradise the swashing beats of angel wings could be heard. I looked, but blinded by the light of the divine presence my mortal eyes could see nothing. And, probably because I am still a child of Western civilization, I do not know to this very day whether somewhere in that glory and among these feathery wings there could possibly have been trailing along the serpent tails of Quetzalcoatl's Olmec predecessors.

The reader may have been wondering by now concerning the whereabouts of the jaguar in this glorious vision. Well, just as I was ready to return to the world of problems and books, I noticed by my feet a beautifully spotted jaguar. For a moment, I must confess, a touch of fear crept into my spine. Will this animal ever forgive me for what I have done? To my great surprise the jaguar, as if he had read my distorted suspicions, brushed his soft body gently up against my legs. And then, as if to tell me that my story had altogether failed to impress him, he lay beside me and yawned. That was the first time I had seen the full length of a jaguar's tongue.

Fig. 60.—The answer of a friend.

BIBLIOGRAPHY

Abbreviations:
BAE Bull.: Bureau of American Ethnology *Bulletin*
BAE Ann. Rep.: Bureau of American Ethnology *Annual Report*
CUCARF.: *Contributions of the University of California Archaeological Research Facility*, Berkeley

Alexander, H. B. *The Mythology of All Races: North American.* New York, 1916.
————. *The Mythology of All Races: Latin American.* New York, 1920.
Anderson, F. G. "Early Documentary Material on the Pueblo Kachina Cult," *Anthropological Quarterly*, Vol. XXIX (1956), 31–44.
Beals, R. L. "The Comparative Ethnology of Northern Mexico," *Ibero-American*, Vol. II (1932), 93–225.
————. "Relations Between Meso-America and the Southwest," *El Norte de Mexico y el Sur de Estados Unidos.* Mexico City, 1943, 245–52.
Benedict, R. *Zuni Mythology.* 2 vols. New York, 1935.
Benson, E. P. (ed.). *Dumbarton Oaks Conference on the Olmec, 1967.* Washington, D.C., 1968.
Bernal, I. *The Olmec World.* Berkeley, 1969.
————. "The Olmec Region—Oaxaca," *CUCARF*, Vol. XI (1971), 29–50.
Bernal, I., and I. Groth. *Ancient Mexico in Colour.* New York, 1968.
Bourke, J. G. *The Snake Dance of the Moquis of Arizona.* New York, 1884.
Boyd, M. *Tarascan Myths and Legends.* Fort Worth, 1969.

Brew, J. O. "On the Pueblo IV and on the Katchina-Tlaloc Relations," *El Norte de Mexico y el Sur de Estados Unidos*. Mexico City, 1943, 241–45.

Caso, A. *The Aztecs: People of the Sun*. Norman, 1958.

Clewlow, C. W., Jr. "Comparison of Two Unusual Olmec Monuments," *CUCARF*, Vol. VIII (1970), 35–40.

Clewlow, C. W., Jr., and C. R. Corson. "New Stone Monuments from La Venta, 1968," *CUCARF*, Vol. V (1968), 171–203.

Clewlow, C. W., Jr., R. A. Cowan, J. F. O'Connell, and C. Benemann. "Colossal Heads of the Olmec Culture," *CUCARF*, Vol. IV (1967).

Coe, M. D. *The Jaguar's Children: Preclassic Central Mexico*. New York, 1965 (a).

— — — —. "Archaeological Synthesis of Southern Veracruz and Tabasco," *Handbook of Middle American Indians*, Vol. III, 679–715. Austin, 1965 (b).

— — — —. "The Olmec Style and its Distribution," *Handbook of Middle American Indians*, Vol. III. Austin, 1965 (c), 739–775.

— — — —. *The Maya*. New York, 1966.

— — — —. *Map of San Lorenzo, an Olmec Site in Veracruz, Mexico*. New Haven, 1967.

— — — —. *America's First Civilization*. New York, 1968.

— — — —. "The Archaeological Sequence at San Lorenzo Tenochtitlan, Veracruz, Mexico," *CUCARF*, Vol. VIII (1970), 21–34.

Covarrubias, M. *Mexico South: The Isthmus of Tehuantepec*. New York, 1946.

— — — —. *Indian Art of Mexico and Central America*. New York, 1957.

Cushing, F. H. "Outlines of Zuni Creation Myths," *BAE Ann. Rep.*, Vol. XIII (1891/92), 321–447.

— — — —. *Zuni Folk Tales*. New York, 1931.

Daifuku, H. "The Pit House in the Old World and in Native North America," *American Antiquity*, Vol. XVIII, No. 1 (1952), 1–7.

Dibble, C. E. and A. J. O. Anderson (trans.). *Florentine Codex, Book 10*. Santa Fe, n.d.

Disselhoff, H. D. *Geschichte der Altmexikanischen Kulturen*. Muenchen, 1967.

Dorsey, G. A. and H. R. Voth. *The Mishongnovi Ceremonies of the Snake and Antelope Fraternities*. Field Columbian Museum, Publication 66. Chicago, 1902.

Dozier, E. P. *The Pueblo Indians of North America*. New York, 1970.

Drucker, P. "La Venta, Tabasco: a Study of Olmec Ceramics and Art," *BAE Bull. 153*, Washington, D.C., 1952.

————. "The Cerro de las Mesas Offering of Jade and Other Materials," *BAE Bull. 157* (1955), 25–68.

Drucker, P., R. F. Heizer, and R. J. Squier. "Excavations at La Venta, Tabasco, 1955," *BAE Bull. 170*, Washington, D.C., 1959.

Ediger, D. *The Well of Sacrifice*. Garden City, 1971.

Eliade, M. *Myths, Dreams and Mysteries*. New York, 1960.

————. *Patterns in Comparative Religion*. Cleveland, 1963.

Faust, G. T. and J. J. Fahey. "The Serpentine-Group Minerals," *Geological Survey Professional Paper 384-A*. Washington, D.C., 1962.

Ferdon, E. N. "A Trail Survey of Mexican-Southwestern Architectural Parallels," *School of American Research, Monograph 21*. Santa Fe, 1955.

Fewkes, J. W. "A Central American Ceremony Which Suggests the Snake Dance of the Tusayan Villagers," *American Anthropologist o.s.*, Vol. VI (1893), 285–306.

————. "Tusayan Snake Ceremonies," *BAE Ann. Rep. 16*, Washington, D.C., 1897 (a).

————. "The Sacrificial Element in Hopi Worship," *Journal of American Folklore*, Vol. X (1897 (b)), 187–201.

————. "Tusayan Migration Traditions," *BAE Ann. Rep. 19* (1897/98), 573–633.

Fewkes, J. W., A. M. Stephen, and J. G. Owens. "The Snake Ceremonials at Walpi," *Journal of American Ethnology and Archaeology*, Vol. IV. Boston, 1894.

Furst, P. T. "The Olmec Were-Jaguar Motif in the Light of Ethnographic Reality," *Dumbarton Oaks Conference on the Olmec, 1967*. Washington, D.C., 1968, 143–174.

Garcia Payon, J. "Los Monumentos Arqueologicos de Malinalco, Estado de Mexico," *Revista Mexicana de Estudios Antropologicas*, Vol. VIII (1946), 5–63.

Gladwin, H. S. *A History of the Ancient Southwest*. Portland, 1957.

Hatch, M. P. "An Hypothesis on Olmec Astronomy, with Special Reference to the La Venta Site," *CUCARF*, Vol. XIII (1971), 1–64.

Heine-Geldern, R. "Zwei alte Weltanschauungen und ihre kulturgeschichtliche Bedeutung," *Anzeiger der phil.-hist. Klasse, Oesterr. Akademie der Wissenschaften*, Vol. XVII (1957), 251–262.

————. "Das Megalithproblem," *Beitraege Oesterreich's zur Erforschung der Vergangenheit und Kulturgeschichte der Menschheit: Symposium 1958*. New York, 1959, 162–182.

Heizer, R. F. "The Olmec Region—Oaxaca," *CUCARF*, Vol. XI (1971), 51–69.

Heizer, R. F. and P. Drucker. "The La Venta Fluted Pyramid," *Antiquity*, Vol. XLII (1968), 52–56.

Heizer, R. F., J. A. Graham, and L. K. Napton. "The 1968 Investigations at La Venta," *CUCARF*, Vol. V (1968), 127–154.

Hough, W. *The Moki Snake Dance*. Chicago, 1899.

Jennings, J. D. *Prehistoric Man in the New World*. Chicago, 1964.

Jensen, A. E. "Das religioese Weltbild einer fruehen Kultur," *Studien zur Kulturkunde*, Vol. IX. Stuttgart, 1948.

Jimenez Moreno, W. "Mesoamerica before the Toltecs," *Ancient Oaxaca*. J. Paddock, ed. Stanford, 1966.

Joralemon, P. D. *A Study of Olmec Iconography*. Washington, D.C., 1971.

Kewanwytewa, J. *Legend of the Snake Clan* (unpublished manuscript). Museum of Northern Arizona, Flagstaff, 1961.

Kranz, F. M., H. M. Smith, and R. B. Smith. "Amphibians and Reptiles of the Codices and Narrations of the Ancient Mexicans," *Bulletin of the Philadelphia Herpetological Society*, Vol. XVIII (1970), 25–43.

Krickeberg, W. *Altmexikanische Kulturen*. Berlin, 1956.

————. "Die Religionen der Kulturvoelker Meso-amerikas," *Die Religionen der Menschheit*, Vol. VII (1961).

Leonard, J. N. *Ancient America*. Great Ages of Man Series. New York, 1967.

Luckert, K. W. *The Navajo Hunter Tradition*. Tucson, (forthcoming from Univ. of Arizona Press).

Marquina, I. *Architectura Prehispanica*. Mexico City, 1964.

McGregor, J. C. *Southwestern Archaeology*. Urbana, 1965.

Mindeleff, C. "An Indian Dance," *Science*, Vol. VII (1886), 507–14.

————. "Aboriginal Remains in Verde Valley, Arizona," *BAE Ann. Rep. 13* (1891/92), 185–268.

Morley, S. G. and G. Brainerd. *The Ancient Maya*. Stanford, 1956.

Morris, E. H., J. Charlot, and A. A. Morris. *The Temple of the Warriors at Chichén Itzá, Yucatán*. 2 vols. Washington, D.C., 1931.

Morrison, F., C. W. Clewlow, Jr., and R. F. Heizer. "Magnetometer Survey of the La Venta Pyramid," *CUCARF*, Vol. VIII (1970), 1–20.

Nachtigall, H. *Die Amerikanischen Megalithkulturen*. Berlin, 1958.

Nequatewa, E. "Truth of a Hopi and Other Clan Stories of Shungopovi," *Bulletin of the Museum of Northern Arizona*, Vol. VIII. Flagstaff, 1936.

Nicholson, I. *Mexican and Central American Mythology*. London, 1967.

Nowotny, K. A. *Tlacuilolli: Die Mexikanischen Bilderhandschriften, Stil und Inhalt.* Berlin, 1961.

Opler, M. E. "Cause and Effect in Apachean Agriculture, Division of Labor, Residence Patterns, and Girls' Puberty Rites," *American Anthropologist,* Vol. LXXIV (1972), 1133–46.

Ortiz, A. *The Tewa World.* Chicago, 1969.

Otto, R. *Das Heilige.* Breslau, 1922.

Parsons, E. C. "Some Aztec and Pueblo Parallels," *American Anthropologist,* Vol. XXXV (1933), 611–31.

————. *Pueblo Indian Religion.* 2 vols. Chicago, 1939.

Pollock, H. E. D. *Round Structures of Aboriginal Middle America.* Washington, D.C., 1936.

Proskouriakoff, T. "Early Architecture and Sculpture in Mesoamerica," *CUCARF,* Vol. XI (1971), 141–156.

Recinos, A. *Popol Vuh: The Sacred Book of the Ancient Quiché Maya.* English version by D. Goetz and S. G. Morley. Norman, 1950.

Riesenfeld, A. *The Megalithic Culture of Melanesia.* Leiden, 1950.

Rooth, A. B. "The Creation Myths of the North American Indians," *Anthropos,* Vol. LII (1957), 497–508.

Roys, R. L. (tr. & ed.). *The Book of Chilam Balam of Chumayel.* Norman, 1967.

Saenz, C. A. *Quetzalcoatl.* Mexico City, 1962.

Scholes, F. V. and R. L. Roys. *The Maya Chontal Indians of Acalan-Tixchel.* Norman, 1968.

Schroeder, A. H. "Unregulated Diffusion from Mexico into the Southwest prior to A.D. 700," *American Antiquity,* Vol. XXX (1965), 297–309.

————. "Pattern Diffusion from Mexico into the Southwest after A.D. 600," *American Antiquity,* Vol. XXXI (1966), 683–704.

Seler, E. "The Venus Period in the Borgian Codex Group," *BAE Bull. 28* (1904), 353–392.

————. *Gesammelte Abhandlungen zur Amerikanischen Sprach- und Altertumskunde,* Vol. I. C. Bowditch (trans.). Cambridge, 1939.

————. *Gesammelte Abhandlungen zur Amerikanischen Sprach- und Altertumskunde,* Vol. IV. Graz, 1961.

————. *Codex Borgianus.* Mexico City, 1963.

Silverberg, R. *Mound Builders of Ancient America.* Greenwich, Conn., 1968.

Smith, H. M. and E. H. Tylor. *Herpetology of Mexico.* Ashton, Md., 1966.

Spinden, H. J. "New Light on Quetzalcoatl," *Congres des Americanistes.* Paris, 1947, 505–512.

Stephen, A. M. "Hopi Tales," *Journal of American Folklore,* Vol.

XLII (1929), 1–72.

———. *Hopi Journal.* 2 vols. E. C. Parsons, ed. New York, 1936.

Stirling, M. W. "Stone Monuments of Southern Mexico," *BAE Bull. 138.* Washington, D.C., 1943.

———. "Stone Monuments of the Rio Chiquito, Veracruz, Mexico," *BAE Bull. 157* (1955), 1–24.

———. "Monumental Sculpture of Southern Veracruz and Tabasco," *Handbook of Middle American Indians,* Vol. III, 716–738. Austin, 1965.

———. "Three Sandstone Monuments from La Venta Island," *CUCARF,* Vol. V (1968), 35–39.

———. "Solving the Mystery of Mexico's Great Stone Spheres," *National Geographic,* Vol. CXXXVI (1969), 294–300.

Stirling, M. W. and M. Stirling. "Finding Jewels of Jade in a Mexican Swamp," *National Geographic,* Vol. LXXXII (1942), 635–661.

Stuart, G. E. "Who Were the Mound Builders?" *National Geographic,* Vol. CXLII (1972), 782–801.

Thompson, E. H. *The High Priest's Grave, Chichén Itzá.* J. E. S. Thompson, ed. Chicago, 1938.

Thompson, J. E. S. "Sky Bearers, Colors and Directions in Maya and Mexican Religion," *Contributions to American Archaeology,* Vol. II (1934), 209–242.

———. *The Rise and Fall of Maya Civilization.* Norman, 1954.

———. *Maya Archaeologist.* Norman, 1963.

———. *Maya History and Religion.* Norman, 1970.

Titiev, M. "The Religion of the Hopi Indians," *Forgotten Religions,* V. Ferm ed., New York, 1950, 363–378.

Underhill, R. M. "Ceremonial Patterns in the Greater Southwest," *American Ethnological Society, Monograph 13.* New York, 1948.

———. "Intercultural Relations in the Greater Southwest," *American Anthropologist,* Vol. LVI (1954), 645–662.

———. *Red Man's Religion.* Chicago, 1965.

Vaillant, G. C. "A Pre-Columbian Jade," *Natural History,* Vol. XXXII (1932), 512–520, 557–558.

———. Aztecs of Mexico: *Origin, Rise and Fall of the Aztec Nation.* Garden City, 1941.

Van der Leeuw, G. *Religion in Essence and Manifestation.* 2 vols. New York, 1963.

Voth, H. R. "The Tradition of the Hopi," *Field Columbian Publication 96.* Chicago, 1905.

Wach, J. *Sociology of Religion.* Chicago, 1944.

———. *Understanding and Believing: Essays by Joachim Wach,*

J. M. Kitagawa, ed. New York, 1968.

Wallis, W. D. "Folk Tales from Shumopovi, Second Mesa," *Journal of American Folklore*, Vol. XLIX (1936), 1–68.

Wicke, C. R. *Olmec, an Early Art Style of Precolumbian Mexico.* Tucson, 1971.

Willard, T. A. *The City of the Sacred Well.* The Century Company, 1926.

Willey, G. R. *An Introduction to American Archaeology*, Vol. I. Englewood Cliffs, 1966.

Williams, H., and R. F. Heizer. "Sources of Rocks Used in Olmec Monuments," *CUCARF*, Vol. I (1965), 1–40.

Wolf, E. R. *Sons of the Shaking Earth.* Chicago, 1959.

Wormington, H. M. *Prehistoric Indians of the Southwest.* Denver, 1947.

INDEX